Super-Charged Learning

SUPER-CHARGED LEARNING

How Wacky Thinking
and Sports Psychology
Make It Happen

RICHARD J. GIORDANO

Foreword by Benjamin Carson Sr., MD

ROWMAN & LITTLEFIELD
Lanham • Boulder • New York • London

Published by Rowman & Littlefield
A wholly owned subsidiary of The Rowman & Littlefield Publishing Group, Inc.
4501 Forbes Boulevard, Suite 200, Lanham, Maryland 20706
www.rowman.com

Unit A, Whitacre Mews, 26-34 Stannary Street, London SE11 4AB, United Kingdom

British Library Cataloguing in Publication Information Available

Library of Congress Cataloging-in-Publication Data Available

ISBN 978-1-4758-1307-4 (cloth : alk. paper)—ISBN 978-1-4758-1521-4 (pbk. : alk. paper)—ISBN 978-1-4758-1309-8 (electronic)

♾™ The paper used in this publication meets the minimum requirements of American National Standard for Information Sciences—Permanence of Paper for Printed Library Materials, ANSI/NISO Z39.48-1992.

Printed in the United States of America

This book is dedicated to all the fine young men and women, student-athletes, whose exceptional force of will brings them success in their studies, athletics, and lives.

It is also dedicated to Dottie. Because of her ever-present support and encouragement, she helped to made this book a reality. For her, the biblical "it is more blessed to give than receive" (Acts 20:35, KJV) is not just scripture, but a life purpose.

Let me write the songs of a nation,
and I care not who writes its laws.

—ANDREW FLETCHER, 1653–1716,
Scottish writer, politician, and patriot

Contents

Foreword

I F YOU COMPARE the frontal lobes of the brain in humans with those of other animals, it quickly becomes apparent that, relatively speaking, human beings have gigantic frontal lobes. This is the area of the brain where rational thought processing takes place. It gives us the ability to extract information from the past, merge it with information from the present, and project all of this into the future as a plan. Successful people take advantage of this ability to plan and strategize and alter future events. Unfortunately, large numbers of people behave more like animals with small frontal lobes who just tend to react to the environment rather than shape it. Teaching children to use their massive intellectual capacity rather than be victims is perhaps the most important thing parents can do. That is the focus of this book. When reading it, remember that life can be a great deal of fun when you don't take yourself too seriously. There is a great deal of humor in these pages, but its purpose is to focus on the enormous potential innate in each of our young people and how to develop it. Many of the lessons that are taught in this book are lessons that I learned the hard way. One will see that there are many ways to achieve victory in the development of our youth. As they learn some of the fascinating techniques in these pages, their self-confidence will grow and the old can-do attitude that made America into a great nation will be manifested in their lives. There are a ton of different techniques and methods that can be successfully used to develop the potential of our young people, and Making Up Crap

(MUC) is but one of them. There is a lot to be said for common sense and the use of proven methodology to increase potential and confidence. Even if you don't have young people under your tutelage, learning some of the techniques for improving memory and other mental skills can be useful to all of us. Enjoy the adventure you are embarking upon with this unique tool of development.

—Benjamin S. Carson Sr., MD,
emeritus professor of neurosurgery,
oncology, plastic surgery, and pediatrics

Preface

MANY ISSUES come together to define today's public schools, and two have become prominent over the past several years. While perhaps evident at all grade levels, these are particularly in play at the secondary level: middle school and high school. The first is that public school teachers have become mere dispensers of information . . . not truly "teachers." They *tell* students information (lecture), but do not *show* (teach) them how to go about learning it. Also, as schools become larger and more impersonal, another issue arises. Parents find themselves relegated to a nonparticipant status in their children's schooling, not knowing what role, if any, they might play.

Whether these conditions are in place by design or default is not what you will be reading about here. The intent is not to affix blame or deal with the *why* of this circumstance. As annoying as this comment may be, it is true: "It is what it is!" My goal in the following pages is to show you (parents in particular) an easy yet powerful way to handle things as they are, how you can reengage with your children's schooling, and make a BIG difference in how well they learn!

With years of work in public education, both as a teacher and high school principal, I've found that the keys to learning are not often found in complex learning theories, but in some fairly common things. One of these is that as human beings, we have *three* God-given traits that make us who we are. We are all emotional, physical, and visual beings. It is these three traits that give us our ability to learn complex things. What we must do is *choose to apply them* to our learning situations. If this is done, we can become superior learners . . . *super-charged* learners. If that sounds like car talk, it is!

A super-charged automobile engine enables a car to get off the line (accelerate) more quickly, because its engine has more explosion power and thus moves the car faster. In the same way, super-charged learning gets you *off the line* quicker, giving you more learning power and making you a faster learner. The principles are the same for both. It's about increasing the things that go into producing more power, in the car engine and in your brain.

An automobile engine gets its power from controlled explosions (combustion) of a mixture of air and gasoline inside a chamber (cylinder). The power of the explosion determines the power of the engine— bigger explosion = more power. The explosions are made bigger when the quantities of air and gasoline are increased. A super-charged engine does exactly that. The air entering the combustion chamber is compressed, resulting in more of it being forced into the chamber. Similarly, more gasoline is forced into the chamber. When a spark ignites this mixture, a bigger explosion results, translating into a more powerful and faster car.

Super-charged learning works the same way. Your ability to learn depends upon how much emotion, physical sensation, and visualization you incorporate in your thinking. If you *purposefully* force more emotion, physical sensation, and visualization into your thinking, you will increase your thinking power, resulting in more-power learning. Just as a super-charged car engine is more powerful and results in a faster car, super-charged thinking is more powerful and results in faster learning.

The following pages are a kind of road trip, a trip to places where you may have traveled in the past on a vacation or a whimsical weekend getaway. On those trips, other than some nice memories and maybe a suntan, you brought nothing home with you. This trip will be different! When you get back from *this* trip, you'll have returned with something that you didn't have when you started out. You *will* have nice memories, but they will be more than just pleasant reflections on past times. These will be strong, useful, and woven into some new and factual understandings . . . about *you*! They will empower you to become a stronger learner than you ever thought possible, and you'll get there just by *applying* the God-given abilities you were given at birth. The suntan may be absent, but you'll be returning from this trip with the *souvenir* of being a *super-charged* learner!

Acknowledgments

THANKS TO some fine people!

The work that I have done with university student-athletes has been supported by some *terrific* people that I have been blessed to know. New friends and old have generously given me something of themselves, and that has made all the difference . . . not only in these pages, but also in my life.

Dr. M. Grace Calhoun, currently the athletic director at the University of Pennsylvania, gave me my start when she invited me to participate in an N4A conference at Indiana University. Subsequent to that conference, Dustin Swanson, an academic adviser at IU, provided me the opportunity to work with his freshman football players. There have since been many other fine professionals at other universities who have been helpful to me and my work, but these two got the ball rolling. They took a chance on someone peddling a truly goofy idea . . . "*Crap.*" Absent their willingness to take the risk, *Super-Charged Learning* would not have been written.

Jacque Dreher has been a help far beyond what she can know! Through her suggestions, I came to read books and articles that provided me valuable insights and focus. Also, over burgers at McDonald's one day, she provided the inspiration for my inclusion of J. P. Richardson ("the Big Bopper") in my work with student-athletes. She personified the Bopper's song, "Chantilly Lace," and the song has been part of my work with student-athletes ever since. Her joyful enthusiasm has been inspiring!

Matt Revers was introduced to me by Jacque. The three of us, meeting over coffee at Denny's one morning to discuss health insurance, resulted not only in my finding a new friend in Matt, but also in some connections that I could never have accomplished absent his help. It was Matt's lifelong friendship with Dr. Michael Ain of Johns Hopkins Medical Center that brought me into contact with Dr. Benjamin Carson. I am grateful to Dr. Ain for his trust and willingness to pass my work to his colleague, Dr. Ben Carson.

Dr. Ben Carson was willing to meet with me to talk about my book at a time when he was still practicing medicine at Johns Hopkins, a time when his schedule hardly allowed for such a meeting. Through a discussion one morning in his office and his reading my manuscript afterward, Dr. Carson graciously agreed to write the foreword for my book. While he continues to help young people through his own foundation, Carson Scholars, he found the time to help me in my efforts to do the same. I am in his debt for this kindness.

Dr. Gary Sailes has been an inspiration and help from the day we met in his office at Indiana University several years ago. A sports sociologist, professor, writer, and scholar in matters of race relations, he has offered me support and inspiration. His insights and his willingness to share them is what make Gary so very special, as a colleague and a friend!

Emile Pandolfi is another new friend. Having enjoyed his magnificent piano arrangements and performance style for many years, I thought that he could provide readers a unique perspective on the *psychology of performance* . . . transitioning far beyond the athletic field. So I asked for his help. Emile is not only an extraordinary musician and performer, but more importantly, he is a warm and kind human being, always ready to do something nice for people. If you have not heard Emile perform, your life is missing a real enrichment opportunity. Get a Pandolfi CD (EmilePandolfi.com), and you'll become part of a never-disappointed listening audience.

Coach Bill Lynch, head football coach at DePauw University, has been a help to me since I began my work with student-athletes. We met at Indiana University when he was the head football coach there, and I was just beginning my work with his freshman football players. He has remained a friend and supportive colleague ever since.

When I began working with university student-athletes, I established a professional website: www.makingupcrap.net. The website home page contains a photograph of some good friends from Villa Grove, Colorado, Carol and Bill Case. Carol and Bill agreed to be the "stick out" couple on the website, portraying the underpinning definition of "Making Up Crap." These are very nice people, always willing to lend a hand to anyone in need . . . in this case, a friend with a wacky idea!

Dottie Eichhorn has been of immeasurable help to me. As an author herself, she has kept my spirits up during some trying times. What I write in the dedication for this book says it all.

Finally, I wish to express my appreciation to Tom Koerner of Rowman & Littlefield, not only for his decision to publish my book, but for his kind and generous assistance throughout the process.

Introduction

HE SITS AT his tablet-arm desk reading the questions on his psychology midterm examination, and in the pit of his stomach he feels the terror of what he had previously feared . . . he's woefully unprepared! He's beginning to panic! How could he have spent *so* many hours studying only to come up so short?!

What destroys his confidence by the second is that there are *so* many questions asking him to define and explain structures in the human brain. "Hippocampus, amygdala, cerebellum, hypothalamus" . . . too many of them! He spent *hours* reciting the definitions to himself, writing them down, repeating them over and over. But now he can't dredge up *any* of them! He knows that his panicked state is making it worse, but he can't get over that he is not in control and may *bomb* this test!

You're probably saying, "Been there . . . done that!" Like this poor fellow, you may have spent *so* many hours only to remember *so* little information. And the problem is not that you did not spend enough hours studying. It's that you studied hard . . . but you didn't study smart! The *memo* that it's not how *long* you study but how *well* you study somehow did not reach you!

Super-Charged Learning is about how you can change that, how you can study and learn "smart," in a formal education setting or in your everyday life. It's about becoming an efficient learner by using a no-brainer strategy, one that minimizes the learning time while maximizing the amount learned. It relies *not* upon your IQ or your verbal abilities, but simply on the characteristics that all human beings possess. By nature, we are all *emotional, physical,* and *visual* beings. The trick is *choosing* to apply these human (genomic) traits to the things we want to learn.

A birthday card displays the uniquely creative power that humans, like no other creatures, possess. On the front of the card is a photograph of an elderly couple looking out over a beautiful lake. The man is pointing outward onto the lake and says to his wife, "See that piece of land that sticks out into the water out there? Scientists have a *technical* word for that kind of formation. They call that a stick-out!" (Inside the card is written) "Another year older . . . another year closer to making up crap!"

This senior gentleman's made-up explanation is a poignant portrayal of what sometimes occurs through aging . . . how abilities to think clearly can diminish with age. Explaining things in unrealistic, absurd (wacky) ways can result. In this greeting-card example, the elderly gentleman resorts to silliness, absurdity, nonsense ("crap") to give meaning to his world. *Crap* is not an obscene reference, but one that refers to things that simply have no foundation in reality.

In the midst of this humorous thinking there is a hidden message, a powerful one for learning. If you associate wacky things with what you try to learn, learning happens, and it is almost automatic! By simply *making up crap,* you learn things quickly, efficiently, and hold on to what you've learned over very long periods of time. As silly and simple as this may sound, it works!

In the pages that follow, you will see how you can *easily* increase your ability to learn new information and remember it all. You do it by using your emotional, physical, and visual abilities in Making Up Crap (MUC)—thoughts that are silly, goofy, and absurd, with no foundation in reality. You will learn how and where MUC gets its power, and how it is used by elite college athletes as well as by performers in the entertainment industry. Athletes are *central* in Making Up Crap because some very powerful principles of sports psychology are woven into the MUC learning dynamic, adding additional learning/remembering power.

Finally, if you are a parent, you will learn how to help your children learn . . . easier, more efficiently, more powerfully. You will give them an advantage that even their teachers cannot provide them. You will *super-charge* their learning! An added bonus is that you will find *yourself* learning, right along with your children! "Something for nothing" is not a real-world phenomenon. But this is about as close as you can get!

There is one more remarkably unique quality about Making Up Crap: It has *nothing* to do with IQ . . . high, low, whatever! So if you've convinced yourself that you, and perhaps your children, are just *not smart enough* to learn complex things, you will have to find another excuse! The keys to unlocking *super-charged* learning are in the following pages. All you need to do is read on, and open up to the possibility that goofy, silly, and absurd thinking might just help you, and your children, learn like never before! And it's as simple as making up crap!

A Necessary Addendum

Three people provide an operational focus for Making Up Crap. Their views of how things *ought to be* underpin the MUC strategy, hopefully making it something that will have lasting value for you and your children.

Andy Stanley (pastor, North Point Community Church, Alpharetta, Georgia): "Sometimes people accuse me of not being a deep preacher, being like 'he's not very deep.' And the reason they don't think I'm very deep . . . and I understand this . . . the reason they don't think I'm deep, is because I'm *clear*"[1] (emphasis added).

Dr. Benjamin Carson Sr., MD (emeritus professor of neurosurgery, oncology, plastic surgery, and pediatrics): "In my years as an academic physician, I have had the opportunity to hear many lectures by individuals from all over the world. Invariably, the best talks are not the ones that use complex terms and theories to demonstrate how brilliant the presenter is. Rather, the very best, most profound lectures are the ones that can be easily understood—even by those who are not experts in the field."[2]

Rudy Giuliani (former mayor of New York City): "Words are extremely important to me. I love to read and I love language, the sheer pleasure of words in the right order. Choosing one word over another is an important act."[3]

In the chapters that follow, the intent is to provide you some new tools for super-charged learning. Clear communication, understandable language, and well-selected words have been the focus. If it all comes together as intended, you will be surprised at the success you and your children will experience in learning new things!

Notes

1. Andy Stanley, "The New Rules for Love, Sex, and Dating (Part 1): The Right Person Myth," sermon, North Point Ministries, Alpharetta, Georgia, May 1, 2011.
2. Ben Carson, MD, *America the Beautiful* (Grand Rapids, MI: Zondervan, 2012), 122.
3. Rudolph W. Giuliani, *Leadership* (New York: Miramax Books, 2002), 195.

When We Were Children . . .
On Being *Out There*

Childlike Behavior

LEARNING IS not child's play, so what does "childlike behavior" have to do with the serious business of learning?! Read on, and you'll see how things about young children, the ways they experience life, are the things that help us learn, not only as children but throughout our entire lives! "Try to remember the kind of September, when you were a tender and callow fellow."[1] "Try to Remember," popularized by the Brothers Four vocal group in the 1960s, suggests that the innocence of youth is a life-view worth maintaining as the advancing years take a toll on one's spirits. The lyrics summon the listener to think of a time when he was not so sophisticated in the ways of life. Being a "callow" fellow meant being immature and inexperienced, as callowness is related to age; the younger you are, the more callow you are. Children are then the most callow of all, and the younger they are the more they give expression to their immaturity and lack of experience.

For a moment, try to remember what it was like when you were but a very small child, long before you had any of the experiences that made you the person you are today. Remember what it was like being *out there*, being truly innocent, when nearly *everything* was a first-time experience. The songwriter's ballad portrays the warmth of human experience. Michael Williams's song, "Catch Another Butterfly," is like that: "Do you remember camp-outs right in your own backyard, wondering how airplanes could fly? And the hours spent just playin' with a funny rock you found, with crystal specks as blue as all the sky."[2]

If these lyrics bring to mind some of your childhood experiences, it is certain that they come back to you not in words, but in *pictures*, *emotions*, and *physical experiences*. You bring them all back by *being* a child again, and reexperiencing what you experienced at that time, as the child you once were! If you are a child who grew up in a city in the 1950s, you might have had an experience similar to what many children of that era can remember, roller skating on the sidewalks that fronted your neighbors' houses.

You see yourself gliding unsteadily on the sidewalk with cars rushing by on the street, *right next to you*! You feel the grittiness of the metal skate wheels on the smooth, concrete sidewalks. You *feel* your fingers turning the difficult butterfly-shaped skate key to tighten the metal clamps at the toe of the skate to the leather sole of your shoe. (Your mom never liked these skates; she said they ruined your shoes!) You see and feel your hands tightening the coarse, leathery strap holding your heel to the metal backplate of the skate. Perhaps you can recall some of the emotions you felt way back then, emotions rising in a little boy while he rested on a neighbor's concrete steps, gazing into a clear, blue summer sky.

You will remember, whether through roller skating or some other summer activity, that summertime during your childhood seemed to have been an endless time. Going back to school in the fall was an *eternity* away. You never thought about it until maybe late August, when you and Mom bought the new pencil box and other assorted school supplies. As a child, your job was simply to experience and enjoy everything that may have come along throughout the day. "Simply" means purely sensory: feeling, touching, hearing, tasting, and smelling everything encountered! As you reflect back on those days today, your clearest memories are those wrapped in your childlike, sensory-rich experiences.

As an adult, it's likely not often that you allow yourself the luxury of being totally *out there* (100 percent sensory) anymore. Too many people send you signals that this kind of behavior is childlike, and not at all "adult." As an adult you are not supposed to behave as a child, but *be* adult! Biblical truth: "When I was a child, I used to speak like a child, think like a child, reason like a child; when I became a man, I did away with childish things."[3] You should not *see, experience,* or *feel* as a child does but should contain these traits within an "adult" context. That's a lot to give up! It's also not a good idea for those who believe that there remain things that need to be experienced in this way, *learned.*

Do you notice how exuberant children are and how anxious they are to learn new things? "Wondering how airplanes could fly?"[4] Do you also notice that as people age, this exuberance diminishes? Many of the older people you know have likely lost much of their youthful exuberance. They also seem to have misplaced their desire to learn new things. You have probably had the experience of trying to engage an older person in a discussion only to find that the person has absolutely *no* interest in knowing *anything* about the topic. When this happens to you, it might be well to reflect on one of Gary Larson's *The Far Side* cartoons. A little boy raises his hand in class and asks his teacher, "Teacher, can I leave now? My brain is full!" Sometimes it seems as though people truly believe this *full-brain* theory, and that if they tried to learn too much, well just maybe their heads would explode. Dr. Ben Carson, professor emeritus at the Johns Hopkins Medical Institutions, says it this way: "First, we cannot overload our brain. This divinely created brain has *fourteen billion* cells. If used to the maximum, this human computer inside our heads could contain all the knowledge of humanity from the beginning of the world to the present and still have room left over."[5]

So just what does this childlike, *out there* sensory stuff have to do with education, and about learning? It's this: learning and remembering, basically identical concepts, come about largely through visual, emotional, and physical pathways—not linguistic pathways, words. We *receive* information through linguistic pathways (words), but we *remember* information through sensory pathways—visual, emotional, and physical. We are sensory learners first, with the words being attached afterward to serve as symbols of what we learned.

Think about what occurs following the birth of a baby. The baby comes out kicking and screaming. No formal language is used, and yet the baby is communicating quite effectively. As the baby grows, it expresses itself exclusively by means of sound and movement to communicate comfort, discomfort, and more. It also *learns* to *associate* right and wrong responses to the signals it puts out. If a diaper change is needed, it cries. When the change occurs, it stops crying. It has *learned* how to communicate exclusively by associating its crying with the change that will likely ensue.

All of the baby's learning is tied to and dependent upon its sensory capacities because formal language skills are not yet in place. It makes an action (crying), and then associates its like or dislike of the result (having a diaper change, or not) with the action. Likely, the baby *learns* that crying will result in a diaper change. The learning that the baby has accomplished occurred in the absence of any *formal* language abilities, and completely by means of emotional and physical pathways.

Eighteenth-century German philosopher Immanual Kant stated the thesis that human beings are sensory learners first and foremost succinctly: "*All our knowledge begins with the senses*, proceeds then to understanding, and ends with reason. There is nothing higher than reason"[6] (emphasis added). If Kant is right, then our human genomic capacities for physical sensation, visualization, and feeling (emotion), the ones perhaps strongest in young children, are the key means to how we learn and remember. If we can revisit these childlike attributes on a volitional basis, we can facilitate learning more strongly.

Atomic Learning!

While beginning life absent *formal* communication skills, human beings are nevertheless capable of rudimentary communication through their in-dwelt sensory capacities. As formal schooling commences in places away from their home settings, children are instructed that *words* are the fundamental basis of learning: vocabulary acquisition, sentence and paragraph structure, writing and speaking skills, and more. In today's schools, it is axiomatic that language-skill development be afforded foremost priority. This is a quite reasonable approach, but it can result in some unintended consequences.

Communication skills are of immeasurable value for the acquisition of knowledge for oneself and for the impartation of knowledge to others, but they are *only* that. While a person may possess superlative oral and written communication skills, assuming the concomitant presence of knowledge would not necessarily be a very good bet. Ignorance, and stupidity, are quite common phenomena in contemporary society, and both are frequently manifest by those who are reputed to be the very *best* communicators.

A painful example of this is what one often hears when listening to political speech-making. All too often, nowhere in the well-crafted and delivered address is *anything* of intellectual substance or integrity to be found. The words may be wonderfully delivered, inspirational, and even motivational, but simultaneously absent even a modicum of cogent thought. The reason the words *sound* right is because the speaker infuses large quantities of the emotional, physical, and visual into the delivery. The power of these three is what locks what is said into a listener's mind, even when the content of what is said is either vacant or fraudulent.

It would be inappropriate to suggest that a person should leave school with poor or deficient language skills. Such skills are an essential tool for acquisition and expression of learning, but they are not the *core* ingredients in the dynamic of learning. This *core* is but a simple formulation made up of our childlike sensory skills: the visual, the emotional, and the physical. We somewhat return to an "intermediate area of experience," as described by Dr. Henry Coppolillo.[7] This is the childlike area of make-believe, made-up stories, and fantasy events. While seemingly something that we might wish to outgrow, this ability has strong implications for acquiring and retaining information, learning!

The creativity expressed by the very young provides a powerful force to their learning, and yet most people lose this power early in life. Dr. Ben Carson sums it up:

> Developmental psychologists now estimate that 98 percent of babies are born with creative ability. When we ponder this theory, it makes good sense. What else can infants do all day except lie

around and use their imagination? From their first moments of life, babies have needs. They must creatively develop ways of communicating their needs to parents through movements and noise. These same developmental psychologists estimate, however, that less than 5 percent of us have remained creative by age eighteen.[8]

Synergistic thinking, to be addressed in chapter 4, is a strategy for grabbing onto information and holding it over time, *learning!*

This kind of learning is all about *volition,* willfully making a choice. All you have to do is *choose* to learn this way. It is a tactic that calls upon you to *choose* to apply your emotional, visual, and physical senses to whatever you want to learn. And because these three senses are so very powerful in *making* you learn, *atomic learning* is an apt description!

Do Not Touch!

As stated, learning is most powerfully accomplished by applying the tactics children use as they begin to explore their worlds: the visual, physical, and emotional. If you're not convinced that these traits are at the foundation of learning, here's a true story about how children learn through their senses first, and words afterward.

A man, in his mid-sixties, was having a conversation with his favorite uncle, Uncle Joe. Uncle Joe reminded him of an event that took place back in the early 1940s, when the sixty-year-old man was perhaps two or three years old. Uncle Joe had just finished spray painting the fender of his 1939 Plymouth, which his little nephew was watching with rapt attention. Uncle Joe told the man that after he finished a fender, he looked directly at his little nephew (him) and said, "Don't touch, it's *wet!*" No sooner had the words left Uncle Joe's mouth than the little boy placed his finger *directly* onto the wet fender.

The little boy learned two lessons that day: first, he became familiar with the concept of anger. Second, he learned the concept *wet.* He now had a connection between the word and the concept. "Wet," just after his uncle spoke and before he touched the fender, had no real meaning for him regarding a painted surface. However, as he touched the fender, three things happened to solidify the concept with reality: (1) he *saw* his finger slide on the sticky surface; (2) he *felt* a cool and sticky substance on his finger; and (3) he experienced the emotion of his uncle as he strongly *encouraged* him to remove his finger from the fender. He acquired knowledge (learned) quickly! Perhaps this man's uncle might have wished for more of a linguistic learner as a nephew, but then that was not a possibility for his nephew at the time, or probably for any child of that age.

It was through purely graphic and sensory means that the little boy associated the concept with the word. And here's the interesting thing about this story: this mid-sixties man, years removed from the time the event took place, *still* had an image of this event within his mind. As his uncle revealed the details of that long-ago summer day, he still had a strong recollection of it happening, just as his uncle described it. The power of suggestion? Maybe, but probably not, and here's why.

The man's uncle revealed the details of the story as they have been recounted here, explaining the entirety of the scene that took place in the garage years earlier. The *details* are all that the man should have remembered, if his memory of them was just a function of his uncle's power of suggestion. You could even make the case that his uncle was just a prankster and that this event never really happened. His "memory" of it and his ability to recount it years afterward was merely a case of his uncle's *words*, since the event might not have ever taken place. But here's the clincher! Not only does the man remember the details of the event as told by his uncle Joe, he remembers things about that day that Joe did *not* reveal to him as he told him the story, *so* many years after the events took place.

Today the visual, physical, and emotional things he experienced over sixty years ago when the event took place all came back! He remembers that touching the fender happened in the summer and that the garage doors opening onto the alley were wide open, and it was a *very* hot day. The color of the car was maroon. He can remember his uncle cleaning the paint off his finger with a rag soaked in a smelly chemical. And, most of all, he remembers his uncle explaining to him, after his anger had abated, why he said "Do not touch!" and why what he did made his uncle angry. He also remembers walking home through the alley feeling badly about what he had done.

Not one of these things was told to him by his uncle, and yet he remembers them as though they had just occurred, although over sixty years had passed since the event! Dr. Ben Carson provides a possible explanation for why this man remembers what happened so long ago in that garage, including things that were not even told to him by his uncle: "We also know that the brain retains everything. I often use a saying that the brain acquires everything that we encounter."[9] What that little boy experienced in that long-ago time *never* left his memory! Dr. Carson explains that it is possible to touch, with a probe, specific areas of the human brain and that this touching causes a person to instantly recall what is stored in that place. The difference between what is remembered and what is not remembered has to do with two issues: the first is *where* the information is stored, either in the subconscious or the conscious. Second is *how the content was learned* initially. What this suggests is that one's capacity for remembering is infinite! But more important than an enormous memory capacity is the fact that remembering is highly related to a human's sensory abilities and how they are actively engaged to remember things.

One thing is certain. The more powerful the sensory stimulation is, the greater will be the strength and longevity of the memory. Much of what you experience is stored in the subconscious and not subject to *volitional* recall. This is because you make no specific effort to keep it current in your conscious memory. Keeping things in your conscious memory is a volitional act; you can make it happen or not. The senses, then, are a powerful strategy for remembering, for holding onto things in the conscious mind. You can maximize learning and remembering if you make a conscious *choice* to use them.

Grow Up?

You've probably heard one person say of another, "He has a good sense of humor." A more accurate statement might be that the person referenced *has* a sense of humor. Finding an adult with a good sense of humor is a far more difficult task than finding a child with one. Young people, and particularly very young children, laugh easily, at themselves, others, and virtually anything around them that strikes them as out of the ordinary.

A child's *sense* of humor is hardwired, only to be gradually but systematically short-circuited as maturation into adulthood takes place over the ensuing years. If you think about it, a substantial part of *being mature* has to do with restraint and composure, hardly contributory prerequisites for maintaining a sense of humor. It is likely true that a child's sense of humor plays a critical role in an overall ability to *be available* for learning, more so than is possible at later stages of development. The lightness of spirit, lack of bodily tension, and openness of a child that accrues from a humor-available outlook on the world is a powerful precursor for learning.

Unfortunately, the act of *growing up* is one wherein what you recognize as funny as a child becomes changed into something you cannot laugh at because it is impolite or insensitive. Sound familiar? The curse of *political correctness*, pervasively destructive to freedom of expression in any society, is even more devastating to a child's freedom to learn. Political correctness takes the teaching of polite behavior to a damaging level of gross restriction of the senses, the very senses so critical for learning. Looking over one's shoulder has a reductive influence on one's ability to look ahead, to learn. It is antithetical to developing and nurturing a sense of humor, and learning, at *any* age.

The emotion of humor in the Making Up Crap process plays a powerfully enabling role in helping you lock onto new information. Attaching a new piece of information to a funny story, a snapshot picture that you have in mind, or a blatant fabrication wherein goofy stuff is associated all form strong memory bonds. Children do this easily because of their *out-there* natures. For older learners, finding humor or creating it to serve a learning need becomes a more difficult task, but one well worth the effort. Reaccessing your childlike mind-set, again being open to the funny stuff around you, reduces some of the maturity-based stodginess too often associated with learning new things.

Getting Back to Childhood

Childhood is a richly instructive example of how you learn. This brief time of life provides an unblemished picture of how the human being, before it becomes *mature*, learns and experiences much of what it comes to know about life. The learning and remembering is accomplished solely with the attributes that the child brings to the situation, unimpacted by the negative external influences that have yet to be experienced by the child.

Children learn new things by using their senses. They see, hear, smell, touch, and taste things that they can then tie in (associate) with the information they already know. Then they can attach labels to the new things—words—now to be used as symbols for the newly acquired learning. This new learning/remembering is first physical, emotional, and visual before it can be characterized and subsequently reaccessed through the means of language.

The human genome contains *all* the physical God-given properties that are the unique possession of every human being, from birth to death. These properties go *far* beyond what any other form of animal life on the face of the earth could ever hope to possess. The capacities to "hope" as well as "believe" are also examples of uniquely God-given genomic properties that lower forms of animal life do not possess. These two capacities provide humans a unique ability to project and to work toward that which is projected. These genomic properties, if purposefully and systematically exploited, give everyone, regardless of age or perceived mental abilities, uniquely powerful capacities to both learn and remember new information.

Resident, while somewhat hiding, in this statement is the real key to all learning—*human volition*, a person's unique ability to *make a choice* to do something. This is perhaps the most powerful learning tactic that human beings possess. Volition lives large in learning, and it is the underpinning genomic-based power of the Making Up Crap learning strategy.

Notes

1. *The Fantasticks*, "Try to Remember," 1960, music by Harvey Schmidt, lyrics by Tom Jones.
2. "Catch Another Butterfly," 1968, words/music by Mike Williams, B. F. Deal Records, Austin, TX.

3. Holy Bible, First Corinthians 13:11, The New Testament, *New American Standard Bible*, Updated Edition (The Lockman Foundation, 1999), 225.

4. "Catch Another Butterfly."

5. Ben Carson, MD, *Think Big* (Grand Rapids, MI: Zondervan, 1992), 206.

6. BrainyQuote.com, Immanual Kant, http://www.brainyquote.com/quotes/authors/i/immanuel_kant.html.

7. Henry D. Coppolillo, MD, "The Transitional Phenomenon Revisited," *Journal of the American Academy of Child Psychiatry* 15, no. 1 (1976): 36–48.

8. Carson, *Think Big*, 224.

9. Carson, *Think Big*, 206.

The Human Genome

What Is It and Who Cares Anyway?

ENOME? Is that Calvin Klein or Levi? Science has clarified many things about our world, but sometimes it seems as if science does as much to confuse as to enlighten. If *genome* is one of those confusing things for you, or if you've not even heard the word, this chapter will give you a simple way to understand it . . . as well as show you what you can do with yours! Yes, you have one, but do you know what to do with it? That is what this chapter is about: not only *understanding* what the human genome *is*, but also how your tapping into yours provides you an extraordinary ability to learn better than you ever thought possible!

What It Is

One way to picture a genome is to ask some questions about some everyday things. For example, what makes a fish a fish and not a cow? Sounds like an absurd question to be sure. But the answer to this question lies in knowing that one of these creatures is different from the other because of things it has but the other does not. Also important to recognize is that each creature has a unique *form and function* . . . what it looks like and what it does. A fish lives in water and extracts the oxygen it needs to live from the water in which it swims, through its gills. A fish is called *cold-blooded*. It has no internal thermostat to control its body temperature but takes on the temperature of the water in which it swims: cold water = cold fish! And, as everyone knows, a fish swims by means of fins and a tail that propel it through the water. A cow lives in an atmosphere of air and extracts the oxygen it needs from the air through its lungs. It is called *warm-blooded*; its body temperature is determined by its own internal mechanisms, its own personal thermostat. Even when it is cold outside, the cow's internal thermostat keeps it warm. Its body temperature is not dependent upon the outside temperature. And while it, too, has a tail, the cow certainly does not use it for locomotion but walks on land by means of its legs; also . . . no fins!

Each of these animals, fish and cow, has what is called a *genome*. Think of the *genome* for each of these animals as the total package of all of the ingredients (traits) that contribute to making the animal what it is, a fish or a cow. The fish has ingredients (traits) that the cow does not have, and vice versa. The combination of all the traits an animal has, and there are millions of them, make it what it is and different from everything else.

The genome is like a *recipe* such as a person would use for baking a cake. A vanilla cake recipe is different from a chocolate cake recipe because of the one ingredient (trait) one has but the other does not; in this case, vanilla or chocolate. But while vanilla and chocolate make one cake different from the other, each cake is a combination of lots of other ingredients: flour, eggs, milk, shortening, and more. Each of these ingredients is essential, in combination with all the others, to make a cake a cake. And while there are a lot of different flavors of cakes beyond vanilla and chocolate, *all* cakes contain many of the *same* ingredients. They *all* contain flour, eggs, shortening, and more. What makes one cake so very different from the others is that it has a *unique* ingredient, an ingredient that the others do not have—chocolate or vanilla. It cannot be both!

It's the same with animals like the fish and cow. Of course, there are a lot of different traits that go into making a cow different from a fish, unlike the case in which just one (vanilla or chocolate) makes the difference in a cake. But the principle is the same. Every living thing is what it is, and not something else, because of its own unique recipe, the combination of all of its ingredients. The combination of all its traits (its recipe) is called its *genome.*

There are millions and millions of these traits for every living thing, and every living thing is uniquely identified by how these traits display, are visible. The human being has almost uncountable traits that no other living thing has, traits that make people uniquely different from all other animals on earth. And getting the maximum benefit from all these human traits, all found in the human genome (recipe), is like squeezing the juice out of a big, ripe orange!

Unfortunately, some people are not using their genomic traits to their maximum advantage, or using them at all. They are just not "squeezing the juice out of their oranges!" Everyone has these powerful traits, a genome full of them! But it's up to each person to *exploit* them for a maximum benefit. This book is about just *one* category of these uniquely human traits: those that give us the ability to *learn* . . . and *remember* what is learned!

A *Dirty* Word?

The word *exploit* often generates a negative mind-set today. In American culture, infused with the curse of *political correctness* as it is, it is often taken to mean one group or person doing something bad to another. It has become another of those words, like *discrimination*, that has gained a bad rap. In point of fact, this understanding is a distortion of the meaning of *exploit*. So before getting into the specifics of the human genome and its relevance to Making Up Crap, the truth of this word's definition is a good place to begin.

First, *exploit* is intended to depict *precisely* what the term is defined to mean: (1) to turn to practical advantage; utilize for profit; (2) to use selfishly for one's own ends. Oops! . . . there's another PC term that has a *very* bad connotation, *selfish!* The meaning: devoted or caring *only* for oneself. Are *exploit* and *selfish* appropriate here? Yes, they most certainly are! If you think of the human genome as *your* personal big, ripe orange, you should definitely squeeze every ounce of juice out of it, drink it down, and enjoy and benefit from it all by yourself . . . and *for no one else!* There's a whole lot of terrific *nutrients* inside that orange, and you'd be foolish not to take and use them all, *just for you.* But know this: it is unlikely that anyone around you will be doing what you're doing, enjoying their orange as fully as you are enjoying yours. But even in the event that they might be jealous of you, they need not be tempted to take your orange from you . . . but merely to squeeze their own. Still, you will probably be alone in this squeezing venture, the standout in the crowd. The reason that you'll be the Lone Ranger is that most people don't know that they even own such an orange, let alone that they should be squeezing it.

That's what this book is all about: getting the word out so that *everyone* can squeeze his or her own orange (*use* what's in your genome recipe!) . . . simply by Making Up Crap. And while this information is of perhaps the greatest value to parents who want to help their children in their schooling, *everyone* can benefit from this extraordinary "juice." In fact, everyone gets *juiced* when they exploit their own personal *genomic orange.*

Inferior yet Superior

It is likely that most people know that the human being is at the top of the list of all animals on earth in terms of brain power. As mentioned before, this is defined largely by the ability to think, learn, and remember. However, the *mechanics* of how you think, learn, and remember may be less well known. The brain is the anatomical structure wherein thought and learning reside, but thought and learning are a manifestation of the *mind*, through which the activity of the brain is *expressed.* How the mind works is a complex story of interwoven neurons, synapses, and electrochemical interactions, and, as such, it goes far beyond the boundaries of this discussion. However, understanding these complex issues is not required to know that a human's ability to learn and remember is highly reliant upon *physical, visual,* and *emotional* abilities. But these traits are also possessed by many of the *lower* animals: cats, birds, and dogs, for example. And by some measures, humans are substantially inferior to their lower animal counterparts.

Our human *genomic makeup* (the recipe of ingredients/traits we have), even when appearing to be inferior for performing a specific task, still gives us the ability for *superior* performance. To show this, three comparisons will be made between the human being and *lower* animals. First, a contrast will be made between the human genomic equipment (recipe) and that of a house cat, highlighting *physical* differences. Next, wild birds will highlight the *visual* differences between bird and man. Finally, comparing the domestic dog with the human being will clarify the differences in the category of *emotion*. As a starting point, it is important that there is agreement that these lower animals (cat, wild bird, and dog) *all* possess the three genomic traits being discussed: physical, visual, and emotional. They do.

Here, Kitty Kitty!

The most popular pet in America today, appearing in approximately ninety million households (34 percent of all households), is the domestic cat. Archaeological findings suggest that the domestic house cat first appeared about twelve thousand years ago in the Middle East. Its domestication and subsequent ongoing relationship with man took place somewhat by accident. The story goes that dogs were domesticated long before cats because they were a big help in a hunting-based society. When man shifted to an agricultural lifestyle and began storing up the grains he grew, cats wandered in and took up residence with him, happy to find a supply of mice within the grain storehouses.[1] Such were the cat's beginnings, and to this day farmers rely upon these furry friends in place of the less tidy traps and poisons.

Cat people know the warmth and benefits of having their kitty snuggled warmly on their lap and are quick to point out that this is something that dog owners simply cannot enjoy. And cats continue to serve the pest-control function for which they initially gained favor. Anyone watching one of these *mousers* is amazed at their quickness and dexterity in catching prey. And they are just as nimble of foot when *they* are the prey.

Outside a public library on a small-town street in mid-America, a cat wanders lazily out into the middle of the street, only to spot a dog sitting on his front porch . . . watching it with great interest. The cat stops in its tracks! The dog shoots off the porch like a rocket, running full tilt at the cat. The cat makes one evasive feint to the right and then breaks left, going past the dog in a flash and up onto the porch where the dog had been lying. The dog manages a clumsy about face and bolts back toward the porch a few feet behind the cat. The cat flies through the pickets extending downward from the railing in one graceful bound, shoots across an alleyway, and races up an oak tree even before the dog has yet turned to get off the porch.

Piece of cake; no serious challenge for the kitty. All of this drama enfolds in perhaps ten seconds, if that long. Observing such a display of sheer speed and agility, one can't help but be humbled by this *lower* animal. Mentally playing out this scenario with a *man* in place of the cat would have had a different, bordering on humorous, result. If the dog had not chomped the man's leg before he got past the middle of the street, he'd surely have had him before he reached the porch. Had the man been so lucky to get there, he'd likely be *lunch* before reaching the porch railing. Even if he made it over the railing, his tree-climbing ability would prove problematic in escaping the excited Fido!

Anyone who has watched Animal Planet has seen the remarkable speed and physical prowess of the cheetah, a distant relative to the house kitty. A cheetah can accelerate from zero to sixty miles per hour in just three seconds![2] To put that into perspective, one of the fastest automobiles in the world is the Ferrari 458 Italia, which gets to sixty miles per hour in three seconds also.[3] It's not unreasonable to see your pet cat as a mini Ferrari. And your kitty can corner more quickly and tightly than the Italian version.

Man is not included in these data because he comes nowhere near reaching sixty miles per hour over *any* distance. The take-away from this comparison is that the human being is completely outclassed by the cat, and most other animals where *physical ability* is the calculus.

Most people would say that humans are intellectually superior to lower animal forms, largely because of their larger brains (cerebral hemispheres). But while this is typically the case, it is not true across all animal species. For example, birds have much larger cerebral hemispheres than humans when brain weight is compared to body weight.

A hummingbird has a 1:12 brain-to-body weight ratio as compared to a human, which weighs in at 1:40. But the relative brain-to-body weight may not be as important a factor as is *brain differentiation*—how the brain is constructed and organized to perform specific functions. This measure often trumps other measures such as weight and size.

Watch the Birdie!

Vision is one area wherein birds outperform humans in strength-of-expression criteria. As an example, many birds have been found to have two areas of the retina that are specialized for detailed vision. One area is for looking to the front and the other for looking to the side . . . sometimes *at the same time*![4] Humans have a retina that allows us to focus on one place/thing at a time, and *only* one. And that means that we can look only in one direction at a time, either to the front or side, but not simultaneously in both.

Another interesting comparison between birds and humans is seen in memory capacity. Ever forget where you placed your car keys? Birds don't have that problem. "Of course," you say, "they don't *have* car keys! But they *do* put lots of things in a lot of places, and they are very good at remembering where they are." A dramatic example displays this. Many of us have bird feeders where we watch our feathered friends take their fill of seeds, fly off, and quickly return for more. In Colorado, the Steller's Jay, Pinion Jay, and Clark's Nutcracker are notorious for cleaning out a feeder in short order, giving other birds hardly a chance at the feed! These birds gobble up dozens of seeds at a time and then fly off. Then, they quickly return to repeat the process. How can they eat so much so quickly and then return for more? The fact is that they are not *eating* the seeds, but storing them away for future use, often in small pockets that they dig in the ground. And when they need this food at a later time, they return to these storage places with about 90 percent accuracy! How do they remember where they put their seeds? Studied observations have shown that these birds have the ability to create powerful (mental) spatial maps of where they place their seeds. They can visually *map* an area of the ground's surface, deposit seeds, and later relocate them within these mental maps. Maps are made up of *vertical* objects in the area: trees, rocks, and other things that are above the surface of the ground, objects that remain visible when winter snows cover the ground.[5] This behavior suggests that birds are *superior to humans* in acute visual discrimination and locational recall abilities.

Sit, Fido!

"People do not own cats . . . cats own people!" This statement, if accurate in describing the way people relate to their feline pets, draws a stark contrast to how people relate to their dogs. For both, there is a degree of anthropomorphism in play, anthropomorphism being the tendency to ascribe human characteristics to animals. Cats, dogs, parakeets, even hamsters can elicit this response from their owners. Some people have a tendency to believe that their pets think and feel as they think and feel, resultantly having similar understandings and perspectives. This is anthropomorphism. However, anthropomorphism aside, dogs *do* have emotions. But to what degree?

A dog can demonstrate his emotions when being petted as well as when his dinner dish comes near. He is clearly happy and displays his pleasure by tail wagging and perhaps through uttering a whine of delight. However, these behaviors are all of a *stimulus-response* nature and are not generated by the dog making a *conscious choice* to behave this way. These behaviors are mere reactions to situations. In short, the dog is *caused* to respond in an emotional manner by a stimulus external to himself (e.g., his dinner dish brought near). He does not *choose* to salivate and wag his tail. He just *reacts* that way.

Those who study animal behavior list two kinds of emotions present in the animal world: (1) the primary emotions, including fear, joy, sadness, and anger; and (2) the secondary emotions, anxiety, jealousy, and shyness. Almost everyone agrees that the primary emotions are present in lower animals because the animals display them. But the presence of secondary emotions remains unresolved. Animal behaviorists suggest that a *theory of mind* would need to exist within a dog in order for a secondary emotional response to manifest, and that this trait is not part of a dog's genomic makeup.

The theory-of-mind concept was introduced in 2001 to mean "being able to infer the full range of mental states (beliefs, desires, intentions, imagination, emotions, etc.) that cause action. Briefly stated, having a theory-of-mind is to be able to reflect on the thoughts in one's own mind and in the minds of others."[6] In a lighter moment in one of his sermons, Pastor Andy Stanley provides his humorous insight on how the *theory of mind* concept relates to dogs:

> The ability to believe is the most powerful force at mankind's disposal. And it's an ability. You know, we don't think of it as an ability because we've just grown up. Everybody can *believe*, but I don't think my dogs have this *ability*. I've had lots of dogs and they just eat and sleep and that's about it. I don't think they have any vision for the future. I don't think they get together and . . . think what could be and what should be. I just don't think they can project into the future. So, this is an ability, and it is the most powerful force.[7] (emphasis added)

For normally functioning human beings, a theory of mind is a given. For it to be operating in lower forms of animal life like the dog is what is in dispute. Simply stated, if you believe that a dog can either project or wonder what another dog is thinking, then the dog possesses a theory of mind. With this understanding, a dog would have the ability to *think* substantively about his place in the world. He would have the ability to ponder, or to contemplate. He would be able think to himself, "Hmmm, I think that little dog over there really likes me! I wonder if I should go over and indicate my interest to her." To date, no one has yet been able to demonstrate that dogs have a capacity to *think* in such theory-of-mind ways.

Volition and Superiority

So how do these behaviors contrast with humans? Regarding emotion that is measured in terms of strength of expression, the dog consistently expresses *far* more strongly than does the human. However, for the cat, the bird, and the dog, the responses displayed by each in the circumstances described are completely uncontrolled by the animal. They express with no restrictions in strength because they have no foundational theory of mind. Were it present, a theory of mind would allow the animal to control the strength of responses; for a dog to bark more softly, for example. But dogs don't do this. They just bark! They have no volume-control ability.

As is the case for all three animals, the dog has no understanding of *why* he feels . . . whatever he feels. He just feels. When a dog expresses anger, the anger is not under his conscious control. The dog does not *think* to himself, "Gee, perhaps biting his hand was a bit over the top. He didn't really *mean* to step on my tail." The power and strength of a dog's emotional response is stronger than that of the human being because it is always expressed without restraint, at 100 percent intensity. Similarly with the cat and the bird, responses are automatic and not subject to control by the animal.

In contrast, a forceful hit by an opponent can trigger a strong emotional response in a football player, possibly resulting in that player becoming extremely angry and instantly animated. However, the nature and strength of his response is under his control. This self-control is what allows him to continue to play within the prescribed rules of the game and not strike out in an uncontrolled rage at the player who delivered the blow. Conversely, this player also has the ability to get himself *psyched up* for the game. He can, by choice, *gin up* strong emotions . . . through his own will. Coaches encourage this ability to get their teams ready to play at a peak performance level.

Football coaches acknowledge that football is a strategic contest made up of the frequently referenced Xs and Os. However, they know that another issue determines the wins and losses, the emotional levels at which their players perform. With this understanding, coaches attempt to get their players performing at what is termed an Ideal Performance State (IPS). The player who achieves an IPS is performing at 100 percent of his ability to perform. He has achieved what sports psychologists refer to as a *white-moment performance*. This is what is meant by an IPS, and it differs from player to player.

If an IPS is to be achieved, an athlete's emotional state must be under the control of *the athlete*, not the crowd in the stands or any other competing thoughts or activities.[8] And the ability of an athlete to rule his emotions and not allow external issues to control him is a learned skill.

Sports psychologists spend hours with athletes teaching and training them in how they can consciously sublimate all outside influences, to focus only on the details of their performance. For example, athletes vary in the degree to which they can shut out crowd noise, not allowing it to influence their performance. Those who can shut out distracting influences and retain a tight focus on their performance tactics are the most successful in competitive situations, especially those wherein a great deal of distraction is present.

To Be or Not to Be . . . It Really *Is* the Question

While making the case that some lower animals are superior to humans in certain criteria, *choice* remains the lynchpin characteristic that is the defining measure of superiority for the human being. This characteristic, uniquely present in the human genome but absent in lower animals, makes *all* the difference.

In the cat-dog scenario, the cat's response is not one of making a *choice* to flee the dog, but that of a strong and immediate *instinctive* reaction. The cat does not weigh any options but instinctively taps into its speed and agility to escape the danger of the approaching dog. It considers no other alternative avenues for protecting itself, and therefore makes no choices between any such options. Actions are mere responses to external conditions.

Were a man faced with a similarly life-threatening situation, say being confronted by a bear, he would certainly know that he would not have the speed or agility to outrun the bear. Most outdoorsmen familiar with bears would say that it would be best to remain still and not make any sudden movements, ones that could startle the bear and possibly initiate an attack. The worst thing to do is to try to run. If he is not too panicked to think, a man so confronted would likely make the choice to try to stay calm and stand still.

Having no ability to weigh the circumstances and possible reaction alternatives, the cat merely reacts with a 100 percent emotional response . . . he runs! But man can choose to run or remain calm. The difference between the cat and the man is that the cat accesses its genomic catalog and comes up with one response: run from predator! Man, while he also has the capacity to run stored in his genomic catalog, also has the ability to *choose* another option. Given the relative weakness of his physical option (running away), he will choose from other alternative means of avoiding injury. *His ability to choose, not merely react, makes him superior to the cat.*

As described earlier, birds mentally file images, like snapshot photographs, of the landscapes wherein they bury their seeds. These are remembered later, enabling a relocation of the seeds. This kind of photographic memory is called *eidetic imagery*, a trait that young children possess in abundance. Psychologists suggest that this trait in school-age children tends to diminish as the capacities for abstract thought and verbal abilities begin to gain expression.[9] But for birds, this trait is a genomic fundamental for survival and remains a strong part of the animal's behavioral repertoire over its life span.

Some human beings achieve remarkable memory feats that *appear* to be the same as the birds'. The yearly United States and World Memory Championship showcases these remarkable talents. Remembering, in order, all fifty-two cards of a deck of playing cards after seeing them revealed one by one, reciting (verbatim) an original composition poem after hearing it read aloud only one time, and sequentially listing over two hundred random digits after seeing them written on a whiteboard are examples of what may appear to be superhuman feats of photographic memory. But, as is detailed in his book, *Moonwalking with Einstein*, Joshua Foer reveals that this ability is *not* an example of eidetic (photographic) memory. It is a *learned* ability.[10] This ability is reliant on a highly tuned form of trickery, not at all the same as that possessed by our feathered friends. So, are birds still superior in sight?

The visual *power* of birds would seem to speak well to their being superior to humans in this ability. However, while birds have a greater capacity for rote graphic recall, man has a capacity for *discernment*, the ability to recognize and interpret fine-line differences. An example would be Sam being able to know that Fred is upset by discerning the emotion that he sees in Fred's scowling face.

It has been demonstrated that birds have the ability to recognize specific individuals within their own species, one from the other. For example, if there were five birds with the names Ted, Bill, Suzy, Fred, and Sally, each of them would recognize each other as distinctly different. They likely do this by scrutinizing the faces of their bird associates.[11] And while not known with certainty, it is thought that birds do this by identifying feather abnormalities or other gross structural differences. However, even as Fred-bird may *recognize* Sally-bird, he has no idea what Sally-bird is thinking or feeling by *reading* her face. Beyond recognizing Sally as Sally, Fred cannot *see* (discern) displeasure, happiness, excitement, anger, or *anything* in Sally's face. If Sally is angry, Fred does not know. If Sally pecks him . . . *then* he knows! Humans, skilled at discerning subtle facial cues, can avoid getting *pecked*. From classroom anatomy dissections of human cadavers, medical students know that facial dissections are among the most difficult. Faces of human beings are a complex labyrinth of intertwined muscles, the collective of which allows for varied expressions. Birds have no such mechanisms for such facial expression.

Exceptions to the Rule

While people do not possess the same *strength* of eidetic (photographic) memory as birds, people afflicted by a condition known as *savant syndrome* are notable exceptions. People classified as *savants* possess the ability to memorize/remember large quantities of information, and *not* by the learned trickery of Memory Championship contestants. Perhaps the best-known example of this phenomenon is Kim Peek. Peek is what is termed a *prodigious savant* (beyond the capabilities of most savants, exceptional). He is portrayed by Dustin Hoffman in the 1988 movie *Rain Man*. Peek's father and caregiver, Fran, provides an insight into Kim's extraordinary abilities in a conversation with Joshua Foer:

> "He's never forgotten anything," Fran told me, including, supposedly, every fact in the more than nine thousand books he has read at about ten seconds a page. (Each eye scans its own page independently.) He's memorized Shakespeare's entire corpus and the scores to every piece of classical music. At a recent staging of *Twelfth Night*, an actor transposed two lines, sending Peek into a fit of such magnitude that the house lights had to be turned on and the play suspended. He's no longer allowed to attend plays.[12]

Hidden within this passage is an additional unique characteristic about Mr. Peek, his ability to focus on *two* separate things simultaneously; his left eye reads a page while his right eye reads another. Recall that some birds have two distinct areas of the retina, allowing a simultaneous focus both to the side and directly ahead.

Another *visual* ability qualifying as an exception to the rule is expressed in the condition defined as *autism*. Autism, similar to savant syndrome, affords those afflicted some quite remarkable abilities, some far beyond the normal population. Asperger's syndrome, defined as high-functioning autism, is the condition manifest by Dr. Temple Grandin. She explains: "I think in pictures. Words are like a second language to me. I translate both spoken and written words into full-color movies, complete with sound, which run like a VCR tape in my head. When somebody speaks to me, his words are instantly translated into pictures."[13]

While Dr. Grandin's heightened visual abilities set her apart in her thinking abilities and, by her own admission, render her somewhat like the animals with whom she works, she is also different in terms of her *emotional* orientation. She is quite forthright concerning her very limited, almost nonexistent, ability to *read* (discern) emotions in others . . . or to express them herself. An example will show how this works. When one person is in conversation with another, each is aware of how what is being said is experienced by the other. For example, if person A inadvertently says something that is obviously stupid, a disapproving look could be expected from person B, and possibly even a comment addressing the stupidity of the statement. Conversely, if person A makes a brilliant observation, the expectation would be that person B would acknowledge it by either a facial expression or complimentary words. By contrast, talking with Dr. Grandin, who neither receives nor responds in such an emotional context, could be disarming! It would be as though she were being blatantly rude! Receiving *no* feedback cues from her as to whether you are right or wrong, insightful or stupid, could make you quite uncomfortable!

Dr. Grandin's circumstance is important because it exemplifies how *very* much people rely upon visual and emotional abilities to both interpret and learn about their worlds, to discern sometimes very subtle differences. In Dr. Grandin's circumstance, her visual and emotional abilities can be defined as "abnormal," clearly a departure from what is commonplace, the "norm." And while these deficiencies have undoubtedly been problematic for Dr. Grandin throughout her life, mostly in her early life, she also stands as a remarkable testimony that deficiencies in biological makeup can be controlled through personal effort, by making conscious choices . . . and with remarkable success!

Dr. Grandin recognized early in her life that her affliction rendered her uniquely able to understand animal behavior, because she saw things as animals saw things . . . in pictures! This ability allows her to write authoritatively on animal behavior. Her book *Animals in Translation*[14] displays her gifts and how they benefit all who seek to understand animals in general, and their pets in particular. Dr. Grandin found strengths within her disability and, through making conscious choices, turned them to her advantage. As an associate professor of animal sciences at Colorado State University as well as a frequent lecturer at autism symposia around the country, she has clearly "squeezed a lot of juice" from her own *genomic orange*.

Combining Resources

Within the human genome reside the powers that, in the aggregate, render the human being a superior being when compared to every other animal on earth. The human genome contains *additives* beyond what lower animals have, ingredients that characterize human superiority. For those familiar with automobiles and their maintenance needs, an oil analogy may prove helpful.

Most all of the major brand motor oils today are nearly identical regarding their chemical makeup. Yet some oils are of a better quality than others. What accounts for the differences is not the chemical structure of the oil but from the *additive packages* different brands contain. Additive packages allow for less friction, extended oil life, and a variety of other positive performance benefits that the chemistry of the oil alone cannot accomplish. The additive packages account for the overall lubricating properties of different brands of oils, and their costs. Similarly, the human being's brain benefits from far more advanced *additive packages* than those of lower animals. One such additive package is *symbiotic synergy*, a package not found in other species.

Synergy is a term describing two or more things acting cooperatively, resulting in the achievement of a desired result. Mom washing and Billy drying the dishes is an example of synergy, in this example, between two people. The result of their cooperative effort (the *synergy* between them) is that the dishes get done. And while there is a collective good accomplished in that the dishes get done, neither Mom nor Billy receives any *personal* benefit from their cooperative interaction.

For the biologist, *symbiosis* is defined as an interaction between two biological species wherein each derives a distinct benefit from the other. An example of this is the *lichen*, a semicrusty-looking material often seen growing on decomposing logs. Their colors are varied and sometimes quite dramatic, ranging from bright yellows to brilliant reds, purples, and dusty greens. Lichens are classified neither as a green plant nor a fungus, but are a combination of a both, a living thing uniquely different from either.

Green plants have the ability to create simple sugars (food) for themselves through a process called *photosynthesis*. But green plants need raw materials (nutrients) to do this. They cannot produce the nutrients themselves. A fungus cannot make its own food like a green plant can, and so it must rely upon something else to make its food—a green plant.

For a lichen, the green plant part and the fungus part work together to do things that neither could do on its own, and each benefits from their cooperative effort. The fungus part breaks down a rotting log and supplies the nutrients needed by the green plant. The green plant part makes food for the fungus. Both gain *individually* through using their specialized abilities. This is an example of *symbiotic synergy*, where synergy and symbiosis work cooperatively together, producing a result that is more powerful than either could obtain if working alone.

While synergy implies *no individual benefit* to either of the cooperating entities, the semanticist might suggest that combining it with *symbiotic* results in a redundancy, because symbiotic also requires a cooperative effort between two entities. However, nowhere in the definition of *symbiosis* is it suggested that the cooperation between two such entities is the result of a *conscious choice* by either of the entities; neither *chooses* to work with the other. In the case of the lichen, neither the green plant nor the fungus *chooses* to cooperate with the other. Obviously, neither has the ability to do so. Human beings *can* make such a conscious choice. *Symbiotic synergy* is a concept uniquely applicable to people, and *only* people.

A Double Whammy!

Genomic power (the total power of *all* of our traits; the entire recipe!) is *built into* each one of us, something like what was described in a conversation about the incredible *powers of a thermos bottle*. One man says to another: "The thermos bottle is the most remarkable thing on earth! If you put something in it that is hot, it keeps it hot. If you put something in it that is cold, it keeps it cold. How does it know?!" Unlike the thermos bottle, we humans *do* know! We have the genomic abilities to decide! Not what is placed within us at our birth, for that is a function of our Creator. But we most assuredly have the ability to decide what we may choose to do with what we are given. We can *choose* how we wish to interpret our world through selective applications of our visual, physical, and emotional talents. The human being, not the thermos bottle, is the most remarkable thing on earth! And the reason is because we have the ability to choose, not merely react.

Super-charged learning is, at its core, *genomic* learning, learning that relies upon our Creator-given abilities to apply our senses of sight, emotion, and physicality . . . by choice. It is a kind of learning unavailable to every other creature on earth, because no other creature has the powerful package of traits wrapped up in the *human* genome.

Making Up Crap is a strategy that combines the power of our *volition* (choice) with the power that flows out of the *symbiotic synergy* of our visual, physical, and emotional powers . . . our genomic powers. The outcome is a learning strategy that maximizes these unique human powers, resulting in learning that, as athletes might say, is bigger-faster-stronger! Through the application of this strategy, you can grasp *bigger* quantities of information, learn it *faster*, and hold onto it (remember it) more *strongly* . . . over longer periods of time. Making a *conscious choice* to address your educational challenges forcefully, combined with a set of tools uniquely designed for the task, affords you a *double-whammy* approach to learning!

Notes

1. David Zax, "A Brief History of House Cats," Smithsonian.com, June 30, 2007, http://www.smithsonianmag.com/history/a-brief-history-of-house-cats-158390681/?no-ist.
2. "Cheetah," NationalGeographic.org, http://animals.nationalgeographic.com/animals/mammals/cheetah/.
3. Zeroto60Times.com.
4. Gisela Kaplan, PhD, and Lesley J. Rodgers, DPhil, DSc, "Bird Brain? It May Be a Compliment!" *The Dana Foundation*, April 1, 2005.
5. Alexander F. Skutch, *The Minds of Birds* (College Station: Texas A&M University Press, 1996), 15.
6. Lynne Soraya, "Empathy, Mindblindness, and Theory of Mind," *Psychology Today*, Asperger's Diary, May 19, 2008.
7. Andy Stanley, "Starting Point: The Series," August–September 2013, Week #7, "Don't Stop," Northpoint Community Church, Alpharetta, Georgia.
8. James E. Loehr, *The New Toughness Training for Sports* (New York: Plume, 1995), 6.
9. Mike Samuels and Nancy Samuels, *Seeing with the Mind's Eye* (New York: Random House, 1975), 43.
10. Joshua Foer, *Moonwalking with Einstein* (New York: Penguin Press, 2011), chapter 5.
11. Skutch, *The Minds of Birds*, 8.
12. Foer, *Moonwalking with Einstein*, 221.
13. Temple Grandin, *Thinking in Pictures* (New York: Vintage Books, 1995), 3.
14. Temple Grandin, *Animals in Translation* (New York: Simon & Schuster, 2005).

CHAPTER 3

Greeting Cards, Obscenities, and the *Stuff* of Learning

THE ESSENCE of *real* learning is acquiring new information and remembering it. It's that simple! Knowing how to *make* it happen, how to "push the buttons" that *cause* learning, is also simple. However, easy as it is, instructing young people on how to do this is most often not taught in schools. While not happening there, it still needs to be done! Children need to be shown that they possess some unique buttons that, when pushed, *make* learning happen for them!

As was explained in the last chapter, human beings are unique in their genomic makeup, having abilities that make them *physically*, *emotionally*, and *visually* powerful! These three traits are the *buttons* that need to be pushed for learning to happen! Finding and pushing these buttons by making choices is what the following pages are about. Where they are, how to push them, and what happens when you do? These are the questions addressed in the following pages.

Happy Birthday to You!

Have you noticed how greeting cards have changed over the past several years? The words and graphics have transitioned from lyrical verse and pastoral pictures to a new breed of *niche* cards . . . some that are rude, insulting, even obscene. This coarsening of the message seems to have proceeded in concert with so many other abrasive trends that have arisen in our culture. Robert Bork made note of this influence in popular music when he contrasted the lyrics of 1930s music with the message of rap "music" today.[1] Not a very pretty contrast! There remain, however, talented writers in both song and verse who do creditable work today, continuing to produce both music and greeting cards that are tastefully unique.

The older couple described earlier in the introduction are an example of the lighter side of what might be called a dual-meaning approach to humor in greeting cards. While one could read some negative, perhaps profane, meaning into the word *crap*, it is quite clear that the intended definition is the nonoffensive one: absurdity, silliness, no foundation in reality . . . *nonsense*! A short story about a 1950s high school English teacher on the south side of Chicago further clarifies the intended context of *crap*.

Mr. Fenster leaned comfortably on his wooden lectern and squinted over the black-rimmed glasses that he wore, observing the raucous behavior of his immature freshman students. Immediately following the bell that rang throughout the school to announce the beginning of class, he rose up and announced in a *loud* voice: "All right . . . cut the crap!" Compliance was immediate!

Although he seemed a bit stodgy in his tweedy coat, everyone respected Mr. Fenster. He was known not only as a very intelligent man but also a highly *proper* man . . . certainly *not* a profane man! As a result, his students understood his strongly intoned suggestion to collectively *shut up*! Mr. Fenster's exhortation to "cut the crap" (stop the nonsense!) in his classroom was intended to restore order so that learning could begin. His statement was delivered with high energy and achieved the result he intended. It *deenergized* a bunch of rowdy ninth graders and rendered them ready to receive his teaching.

Making Up Crap intends the same purpose, but in reverse! Instead of decreasing a student's energy level, it increases it! The result is a unique empowerment for the student. MUC is a super-charging *additive package* for learning. It is all about using and exploiting what is silly, unfounded in reality, nonsensical, absurd, goofy . . . just plain *nonsense*! The behaviors Mr. Fenster tried to stifle are the very ones that, when brought about by choice, give learners a *double-whammy* power to learn.

You Dirty So-and-So

As mentioned, American culture seems to have coarsened over the past several decades. One of the contributors, but certainly not the only one, is the increasingly common use of what used to be referred to as *vulgar language*. And while profanity seems to be ever present in so many conversations today, it remains as it has always been . . . a foolish endeavor. The "why?" of profanity usage provides us a clue into why MUC, while not profane, is such an effective learning tool.

> Primitive man could swear before he could talk! At first he employed inarticulate sounds to *make his intentions known, accentuated by elevated pitch and volume. Even after he acquired a rudimentary vocabulary,* he found that tone and volume alone would sometimes get the job done . . . however inaccurate and non-descript the words themselves might be. From this primitive beginning, he began developing an expansive repertoire and myriad techniques in the art of *swearing*.[2] (emphasis mine)

Profanity has been with us a *very* long time. And as long as it has been conversationally invoked, it has been one of the most *absurd* speech patterns devised by man. This is because none of it makes any sense! By mere definition of the terms used, is it utterly absurd. Those who make a habit of using profane language are often tediously redundant in their word selections, as well as frequency of usage.

Haven't you, at one time or another, had the misfortune of having been within earshot of someone spewing out a litany of profanity-laced sentences, each one punctuated by "f——ing" preceding nearly every other word? And while such usage displays a profound vacuum of intellect, it also reveals something interesting about why profanity is effective and why some people resort to its usage. A summer-camp story is apropos.

A young man, a university student during the school year, worked at a YMCA summer camp as a cabin counselor. In an orientation session early in the summer, he met the camp caretaker, Mr. Doug. Doug and his wife, Nellie, lived year-round on the grounds in a mobile home at the entrance to the camp, and it was Doug's job to take care of maintenance of the camp. While Doug may have been only in his early sixties at the time, all of the camp staff thought of him as the Old Ranger. Always with a cordial twinkle in his eye, he was ever quick with an insightful comment or assessment of the contemporary sociopolitical circumstance. He could speak on *any* topic, and know what he was talking about!

While Doug never finished high school, he was the smartest man anyone in the camp had ever met! Those who knew him best told newcomers how he had read the entire Encyclopedia Britannica once and was on his second time around. Whenever anyone had the opportunity to work with Doug in his shop or on the grounds, they were quick to seize upon it. As they would work at his side, Doug was always willing to answer questions and familiarize them with the wisdom he had accumulated over his years. But in so doing, he was fastidious in his demand that the English language be spoken *properly*. He was a man of few words, but the ones he used were chosen carefully!

On one occasion while working with Doug in his workshop, the young cabin counselor reeled off a string of four-letter functional terms about something that had drawn his ire. Mr. Doug looked at him quizzically and politely asked, "Are you feeble minded?" And while the young man recoiled at Doug's characterization of what he'd said, his ego having been stung as though by a bee, upon reflection he knew that Doug was right! As the Old Ranger explained, profanity is the attempt of a feeble mind to express itself!

A courtroom deputy stands before a witness and says, "Do you solemnly *curse* to tell the truth, the whole truth, and nothing but the truth? So help you God?"[3] (emphasis added). Were this to actually happen, the presiding judge would likely be looking for a new court deputy! However, many people routinely interchange the word *swear* for the word *curse*. Why this transposition of terms occurs is perhaps lost in time. Does *swear* sound a bit less *edgy* than *curse*? Phonetically, the "s" sound is softer than the hard "c." For the purposes of what follows, the utterance of profane language will be called by its proper name . . . *cursing*.

The Maligned Canine

Getting at the *why* of profanity's nonsensical essence could get a bit graphic for the sensitive reader. But if the absurdities of profanity are to be understood, scrutinizing at least one example is necessary. To do this, a common epithet serves as an example, one that is relatively mild in comparison to others that might be used. "You, sir, are a *son-of-a-bitch!*" This assertion could be made for a variety of reasons: the person steals, cheats, is a liar, has evil intent, is immoral, and more. Whatever the classification of wrongdoing, the epithet is clearly *not* congratulatory. If the target for this verbal assault is a woman, as is sometimes the case, such terminology is woefully misguided. The epithet hurled at a woman would certainly not, gender appropriately, be *son* of a bitch. So what does it mean?

The word *dog* has many slang usages, positive and negative, but none profane:

> You lucky dog.
> My dogs are tired and need a good soaking.
> I'm dog tired.
> That posse is dogging us.
> She's a dog. He's a dog.
> That investment was a dog.
> That car's a dog.
> It's a three-dog night.

None of these is a derogatory usage. So why is a *dog*, and particularly a *female* dog, used to connote such an emotional negative? The "son of" add-on doesn't seem to add any clarification. One person calling another a "daughter-of-a-bitch" in the fervor of an argument would probably elicit laughter. But does calling another a *son* of a *female* dog make any more sense? As most know and have had likely the misfortune to hear, those wanting to denigrate a woman often do so by calling her "bitch." But what has evolved lately is that some, likely the *severely* linguistically challenged, now denigrate a man by calling *him* "bitch"! Does this mean-mouthed maligner have a fundamental misunderstanding of secondary sex characteristics?

A Matter of Semantics

The number of profane terms is extensive, but *all* fail to pass the test of intellectual integrity. For example, you have likely been in earshot of an argument between two men and heard one say to the other, "Go to hell!" But why would one man saying this to another think that his emotional assertion adds anything to his side of the argument?! It's like one child saying to another, "Aw . . . your mother wears combat boots!" Neither statement makes sense, either telling a person to go to a bad place or commenting about a close relative's footwear choice. While rude, crude, and abrasive, all profanity is just plain silly! Another example:

> A most eminent clergyman first told me that classic tale of a bishop who was motoring along a highway and passed a stalled truck driver trying to change a tire. The air around the truck was blue from unrestrained emphasis as the man struggled with an obstinate rim. The bishop, eager to assist, stopped his car, got out, and said, "My friend, have you tried prayer?" The perspiring driver looked up and said, "I'll try anything once." So the bishop knelt and prayed, the driver took another whack at the rim, it slipped off easily, and the bishop said, "I'll be damned!"[4]

While a humorous story, even more humor can be found in people who try to be profane . . . while *not* being profane. *Deaconian profanity* exemplifies this kind of silliness:

> *Shoot*, or *Shucks* . . . in place of _____.
> What the *heck* . . . in place of What the _____.
> Son of a *buck* . . . in place of Son of a _____.
> *Freakin'* . . . in place of _____.
> You're full of crap . . . in place of You're full of _____.
> Dumb it! . . . in place of _____ it! (Prevalent in Dutch culture.)
> Oh, hen! . . . in place of Oh, _____! (Again, Dutch culture.)

The story goes that deacons of the early church devised a set of terms that they could use to curse, while not *really* cursing. Whether or not this is true is debatable, but many of these nonprofane terms remain in common use today, allowing those who use them to remain free from profanity. Or are they?

Profanity . . . Why?

The relevance of profanity to learning, especially for younger people, is clarified in a "music" genre in the entertainment industry—*rap*, a multi-million-dollar industry. While *some* of the lyrics can withstand G-rating standards, many of the big-name performers in this medium establish their bona fides by being gratuitously vulgar. And even accepting that some people say they enjoy the sophomoric rhyme patterns of rap, it is the bad language that *makes the sale* to the predominantly young listening audience. Absent the vulgarity, the boringly tedious lyrics would likely fail to attract an audience.

But who among this listening audience could afford to admit this?! This societal dynamic is reminiscent of the 1960s when those purchasing *Playboy* magazine haughtily stated that they bought it for the written articles! Duh! Many years have passed between the time when *Playboy* first appeared and rap music came into being, but human behavior has not changed much in those years. Solomon was right when he said, "So there is nothing new under the sun."[5]

An identical social phenomenon is also in play for that marginal group of "comedians" who trade in profanity in their attempt to be funny. Even if the performer intended to send a message via this "art form," its clarity is diminished or lost within the barrage of vulgarity used to send it. Even so, the "artist" succeeds with the audience willing to listen to this blather! He, all too frequently *she*, succeeds because of the *cringe response* the audience experiences, and that is the goal—shock value!

And while this cringe phenomenon (an emotional *startle effect*) is short-lived, it often results in a lasting *emotional* impact upon those who experience it. Herein hides a powerful educational message: *What makes an emotional, physical, and visual impression . . . sticks!*

Color My World

As a medium for communication among humans, understanding the *meaning* of words is central if an effective result is to occur. If a waiter says *dirt* but you understand him to be saying *eggs*, the breakfast that the chef prepares for you will be a disappointment. For humans, effective communication is reliant upon common understandings of words. But this understanding is always colored by people's emotions, visual abilities, and physical senses. These three are what give words their *experienced* meaning and they form the core of the learning and remembering process . . . for everyone.

This is why vulgarity has such a powerful impact! It creates a *cringe response* in people. When a vulgar word is said aloud, the recognized meaning calls up the emotional, visual, and physical sensation additives, and a *coloring* phenomenon occurs. *Coloring* is what so often *makes* a person understand—*get*—a verbal message. One wanting to send a message of specific content information can use coloring, but it can also be used by one who wants to receive and remember such a message. Performers use this skill in their presentations to their audiences, but it is a skill that is equally powerful for learners who use it in their learning *presentations* . . . to themselves.

The late John Denver told of what he had learned in collaboration with the world-renowned opera star Placido Domingo, in their duet performance of Denver's song "Perhaps Love." Denver said that while listening to Domingo sing the music, he observed how Domingo *colored* each word to bring out its maximum emotional impact on his audience. Denver went on to say that this observation changed the way he sang the words of his songs thereafter, the way he maximized the *emotion* of his lyrics for his audiences. He said that, after Domingo, he sang very differently.

Humans have this same unique capacity to *color* their understandings of information they wish to remember, and to learn and remember more strongly through such coloration. Lower animals, such as the dog, do not have an innate ability to do this because their genomic makeup does not contain the traits that would make this possible. Another *doggie* example makes this point.

Doggie *Understanding*?

Training a dog to sit upon command is a straightforward stimulus-response process. The trainer positions in front of the standing dog and, in *loud* voice, says, "Sit!" As the dog likely does nothing, the trainer then physically manipulates the dog into a sitting position, while again forcefully saying the word, "Sit!" This sequence is repeated until the dog learns to *associate* the word *sit* with the desired response, and sits without the trainer's physical assistance. What gets the dog to get the message and ultimately sit down when he hears the word *sit* is not the *word sit*, but the manner in which the trainer speaks the word. The trainer says the word *sit* in an assertively loud voice. He has *colored* the word.

Anthropomorphism aside, dogs have no ability to understand the English language. However, they do have a capacity to respond to *loudness* and *intonation* (coloring traits) and a trainer's *physical manipulation* forcing a dog into a sitting position; all three are sensory, not intellect related, cues. The dog *associates* the loudness and intonation of the trainer's voice and the physical manipulation of its body with the desired act—sitting. Understanding of the word *sit* plays no role in the process. The trainer might just as well say the word *cabbage*, and the dog would respond equally as well, as long as *cabbage* was used consistently in the training process.

The dog does not *decode* words as humans do to ascertain meaning, but merely responds to an external stimulus. The dog, not understanding word meaning, responds to voiced emotion, and then associates the emotion with the command word. For humans, this is the exact opposite order of events. A person understands word meaning as the word is spoken, and then translates the word (colors it) with emotion. For humans, word meaning is the stimulus to call up emotional as well as physical and visual *colorations*. The critical message for learning is this: These three—the emotional, physical, and visual—add extraordinary power to learning/remembering . . . when they are attached to words.

A Five-Hundred-Pound Gorilla Understanding!

The canine scenario described above and contrasted to the human condition is intended to set the stage for a fundamental understanding:

a "five-hundred-pound gorilla" understanding! Here it is: As human beings, we take in information largely by *linguistic* means. We either read information or have it spoken to us, *words!* And while it is true that we can also be *physical* learners, as in a child learning the concept "hot" by touching a hot stove, these purely physical means are not a central issue for students learning new information, in their formal schooling for example. Most *all* of what children receive from their teachers comes to them in linguistic forms . . . *words!*

Here is the *gorilla-power understanding*: While we *take in* information via words, we do not *learn* information that way. We learn by much more graphic methods—methods that tap into the powers of our uniquely human genome, our visual, physical, and emotional abilities. These are the three "buttons" previously referenced!

Sometimes words automatically push these buttons in you, like when you hear cursing. It happens automatically, as you may recoil at or have a strong feeling of displeasure. However, there are other times when *you* have to make sure your buttons get pushed. Here's an example that will make the point.

When you hear the word *dog*, you immediately form an image in your mind as to the *kind* of dog. It might be a cocker spaniel or a collie, but you immediately *see*, in your mind's eye, a picture of what *dog* means to you. You may feel some emotional response to your image, perhaps warmth, cuddliness, ferocity, or other emotions. These feelings may also cause a physical reaction in you, relaxation at the thought of cuddly, or tension in reaction to ferocity. All of these three are at the center of your definition of *dog*. The word is the *trigger* to your knowing the meaning of *dog*, but *dog* is locked into your memory (as a learned thing) through your "buttons," the ones that are automatically activated, pushed—your visual, emotional, and physical "buttons."

The power in this understanding, a "five-hundred-pound gorilla" one, becomes apparent when you consider what you can do for your own learning abilities if you merely apply your visual, emotional, and physical powers to what you wish to learn, *by choosing to do so*. When you learn by *choosing* to push these three "buttons" in yourself, you learn more powerfully.

Use It or Lose It!

As mentioned, very young children learn about their worlds by physical, emotional, and visual means. Not until they begin formal schooling do these three "buttons" begin to diminish in their lives, through the ways they are taught to experience and interpret their worlds. This happens as children become immersed in their formal schooling, where *words* take on a central role. Staying in touch with the powerful learning mechanisms of the physical, emotional, and visual is what Making Up Crap is about. High-performing athletes strive to stay in touch, to not lose, these childlike abilities. They routinely use these three mechanisms in a sports psychology methodology, ones they *choose* in order to generate powerful emotional, physical, and visual responses in their sports.[6]

The purpose of MUC is to develop an ability to generate, by choice, these three genomic capabilities and use them to increase the capacity to learn and remember new information. Choice is available in limited quantities in lower animals, but it truly lives large in people. Tapping into this God-given genomic gift has extraordinary power when applied to learning. Making Up Crap is a power-packed strategy for squeezing your genomic orange, getting *all* that resides therein, and applying it in a highly self-directed, systemic approach to learning.

A Necessary Disclaimer

With all the discussion of profanity and vulgarity, one might conclude that these are integral to the Making Up Crap learning strategy and that they are necessary and encouraged. This would be incorrect! It is highly unlikely that anyone reading this would not, at a minimum, *recognize* virtually any curse word mentioned herein. You cannot refuse to intellectually *recognize* the terms, but you can refuse to *use* them . . . in day-to-day living as well as in MUC. Profanity was used herein as an example, a most graphic one, of how responses that are emotional, physical, and visual can be caused to occur. This was just an example. Profanity was used to make a point, not to be portrayed as an appropriate example of the MUC process.

MUC can be accomplished with 100 percent effectiveness with absolutely no use of profanity. The key to learning through this strategy is your visual, emotional, and physical nature, and these three attributes of your humanness can be accessed and used completely absent any off-color means.

NOTE: You may have recognized that the five-hundred-pound gorilla description of the Making Up Crap strategy is, in fact, an example of the strategy itself! The association of a five-hundred-pound gorilla with a learning strategy is intended to imply that the strategy has all the attributes of the gorilla. Like the gorilla, the strategy is powerful and imposing, and can physically make a difference if it is unleashed. By using the gorilla association, it is likely that the reader can grasp the power of the MUC process . . . by making an absurd connection between a gorilla and a way of learning!

Next . . . Making Up Crap—how to *get it done*!

Notes

1. Robert H. Bork, "The Collapse of Popular Culture," in *Slouching towards Gomorrah* (New York: Regan Books, 1996), 123.
2. Burges Johnson, *The Lost Art of Profanity* (Indianapolis: Bobbs-Merrill, 1948), 20.
3. North Dakota Supreme Court, Rule 6.10, Oaths, effective March 3, 1999.
4. Johnson, *The Lost Art of Profanity*, 32.
5. Holy Bible, Ecclesiastes 1:9, New American Standard Edition, 792.
6. Dr. James E. Loehr and Peter J. McLaughlin, *Mentally Tough: The Principles of Winning at Sports Applied to Winning in Business* (Lanham, MD: M. Evans, 1986), 60.

Making Up Crap and Synergistic Thinking

What It Is and How It Is Done

NOW THAT you have an understanding of the unique powers you have in the physical, emotional, and visual realms, it is time to put these into a plan that will result in powerful MUC learning. How you work through this process is the focus of this chapter. How do you begin, what are the steps along the way, what does it look like as you're doing it, and what do you have when you're done? These are the issues addressed in this chapter.

At the end, you will have a new way to learn and remember information, even things you thought *you* could never learn and remember! And while there is a diagram included that shows the steps for this process, it is likely that you will not need to reference it in order to use the process. You will *be Making Up Crap* so easily, and with so much fun, that you will wonder why you haven't done it before now. And, you will want to show your children how to do it . . . right away!

Schooling in the 1950s, a South-Side Experience

For children going to school on the south side of Chicago in the 1950s, or any large city elementary school of that era, days were *packed* with stimulus-rich experiences, locking in memories that would endure throughout lifetimes. The sights, smells, and sounds of that time are forever locked onto the mental canvases of these children's lives, painted in brilliant, fade-resistant sensory colors.

Like so many other structures of the time, Van Vlissingen Elementary School was an example of that era of American education. The young lives molded within the walls of that old structure "sets the table" for an understanding of how and why Making Up Crap is such a powerful learning dynamic, one that not only helps you learn, but actually *makes* you learn.

Van Vlissingen School was a four-story structure occupying eight city blocks, constructed with Chicago-common brick and approaching one hundred years of age in the early 1950s. A veritable castle, it was complete with turretlike towers on each of its elevated four-story corners, rising high above and dominating the surrounding neighborhood of modest brick and frame homes. (VV was razed several years ago, but its majesty can still be seen: Google Van Vlissingen School, Chicago.)

The classrooms were all nearly identical to one another. Light-colored hardwood floors that creaked when you walked were punctuated by six rows of black cast iron Y-shaped structures, bolted securely onto the floor. Each iron structure was punctuated with a seat atop the forward and lower arm of the Y, and a desk surface attached to the part of the Y extending behind.

At the front of the room was the teacher's desk, solid oak and centered in front of a chalk-dust-covered blackboard that stretched across the width of the room. Above the blackboard, four things were visible to the students at their desks. In the right corner hung the American flag, to which the children pledged allegiance each morning before class began. Hanging on opposite ends on the wall were pale-color portraits of presidents Lincoln and Washington, casting their ever-watchful stares downward upon the students seated below. Between these portraits was an oak, wind-up, pendulum-type clock . . . the kind occasionally found in antique stores today.

On each side of the blackboard were two wide portals through which the cloakroom was accessed. On the back wall of this long, narrow cloakroom were two rows of black cast iron hooks, one row higher than the other. Upon entering in the morning, children hung their coats, hats, and other paraphernalia on these hooks. (No lockers and combination locks here!) And as children are wont to do, each established possession of his or her own *personal* hook that first school day in September; the upper hooks were for the big kids, and the lower for the little kids. These were commonly understood to be inviolate property! No one *ever* thought to trespass by hanging anything on another's hook.

Hangin' Up Their Stuff:
The Parable of the Hooks

The cloakroom hook was the first stop in the morning as children started school and their last stop as the school day finished. During class time, their personal hook domains held all of the possessions they could not pack with them into the classroom: baseball gloves, lunch boxes, and when it rained or snowed, their metal-clasp rubber boots, placed on the floor below each child's hook.

Children didn't deal with any hook other than their own. They never sought to so much as touch someone else's stuff. Every child in that relic of a building, from September through June, seemingly learned and understood two important lessons: #1, each student *owned* a hook, a place for his or her stuff only; #2 touching what was on another's hook was *not* acceptable!

Those cloakroom hooks provide an insight into understanding the mechanics of how new information is learned, not only in childhood but also over a lifetime. The hooks are the places where you hang *new* learning. You learn new things by *hanging* them on the old and familiar things, things that you already know.

Each of the people, places, and things you have experienced is a "hook," something you know well. When you encounter something new, you learn it and remember it by how it is associated with something you already know, a "hook" from your past. You "hang" the new information on some old information, one of the hooks in your cloakroom of hooks, one of your already known things.

In his sermon "The Comparison Trap," Pastor Andy Stanley suggests that the totality of every person can be visualized as a bookshelf on which all of his or her life attributes are displayed.[1]

Family relationships	Time available in life	Number of friends and contacts
Level of education	Your "unique story"	Dreams and vision for your future
Skill sets	The "unique you"	Health
Talents	Financial resources	Job or career

Pastor Stanley's *bookshelf* is made up of twelve compartments. To expand on this metaphor, consider that each compartment is like the previously referenced cloakroom and that there are millions of *hooks* within each, each having a unique meaning for its owner. For example, the "family relationships" shelf contains hooks representing uncles, aunts, cousins, brothers and sisters, grandparents, and other relatives. Each person (a hook) is a unique entity on which you can build upon, attach a new piece of information. Each person (a hook) has a personality rich in traits: appearance characteristics, unique behaviors, quirks, favorite family stories, and so much more.

This *hook* paradigm plays a big part in the experiential lives of children. Perhaps in your family there was a favorite uncle, Uncle Bob, who was recognized to be a go-getter and the personification of success through his own efforts. His life example may have helped motivate you in your own endeavors . . . to be *like* Uncle Bob. His positive example could have been the hook upon which you formulated/hung your beliefs about work and always making your best effort. He was the model (hook) on which you formed your ideas of what success looked like.

If you wanted to be *like* Uncle Bob, you would *compare* yourself to him, as an ongoing measuring stick of your progress in becoming what he represents to you. You might have associated your behaviors with his, thus getting a measure of your successes.

Pastor Andy Stanley says that "there is no win in comparison."[2] His aphorism is an encouragement not to measure your successes by comparing yourself to others . . . as a *summative* assessment. This is quite different from a child seeing an adult, like Uncle Bob, as a positive role model, a person worthy of emulation. In this circumstance, the child looks up to a favorite relative but is not *comparing* his childlike status to the status of the adult, always coming up deficient. *Summative comparison* is the kind of contrasting that Pastor Stanley defines as futile. The classic poem "Desiderata" (desired things) states this truth: "If you compare yourself with others, you may become vain and bitter, for always there will be greater and lesser persons than yourself."[3]

As harmful as comparison can be, to which "Desiderata" speaks, it can serve as a powerful device in learning new information. Comparing and associating an *unknown* to a *known* thing is a powerful learning tool, especially when you weave the hooks of your past (known things) into learning new things (unknown things).

Well, It's Kinda *Like* This . . .

In 2003, John McWhorter wrote *Doing Our Own Thing: The Degradation of Language and Music, and Why We Should, Like, Care.*[4] Anyone spending time with middle or high school students today recognizes that part of Dr. McWhorter's subtitle, *like*, is annoyingly prevalent in their patterns of speech: "So I was, *like*, listening and she goes, *like*, she's a big fat liar, and so I go, *like*, well then, *like*, don't talk to her anymore! So she goes, *like, I can't!* I go, *like* why? And she goes, *like*, because! So I go, *like*, whatever girl! *Like*, you go girl!"

It seems as though neither person can make a definitive statement, about *anything*! Nothing has its own stand-alone nature but is only defined through its relationship to something else. It's *like* the thing, but not *exactly* the thing, leaving one to wonder . . . "what *is* the thing?!" Overhearing such a conversation makes you want to jump in and ask:

"Do either of you know anything about anything . . . *like*, for sure?!" Semantic dysfunction aside, these two young people have actually hit on a terrific learning technique, if only they knew! It's called *analogy* . . . a truly power-packed learning strategy.

Analogy allows a person to gain understanding of what's *unknown* by comparing it to something that *is known*, by recognizing their common characteristics. Dr. Charles Stanley, pastor at First Baptist Church in Atlanta, Georgia, puts *analogy* into a meaningful context: "In the field of education the 'law of integrality' states that learning tends to be more effective when what we learn is related to other areas of our experiences. In other words, it is easier to learn something that is clearly related to the world around us than something that seems to exist in isolation from the things touching our lives."[5]

The information we know, a hook in our cloakroom, is used to understand something we do not know, resulting in a new knowledge, and a new hook. And because analogy is such an excellent tool for learning, it is also an excellent *measure* of what has been learned: "Research by psychologists on human intelligence and reasoning has found performance on analogies to represent one of the best measures of verbal comprehension and analytical thinking."[6] The Miller Analogies Test (MAT), used widely by university admissions offices to measure the academic abilities of prospective students, makes use of this principle.

Football coaches make use of this hook learning technique with their athletes. As football players must remember large numbers of different alignments and plays, coaches know that analogy is a valuable tool. Bill Lynch, head football coach at DePauw University, uses analogy brilliantly to teach his players to remember plays on the field:

> As a college football coach, we often had our players make up words or phrases to use in calling our offensive signals. In today's game of no-huddle, fast paced football, effective communication is essential. By having our players come up with the code words to use at the line of scrimmage, it gave us a real advantage. The QB could quickly callout the code words that described our run plays or pass protections and our players easily remembered the words because they had *ownership in their origination*. For example, our

pass protections were 50's, 70's, and 90's. Our players called 50's Elvis, the 70's Disco, and the 90's Clinton. Only our players knew the meaning.[7] (emphasis added)

According to Coach Lynch, the players readily associated the 1950s with Elvis Presley as his music dominated in the 1950s. Disco dancing was the rage in the 1970s, and Bill Clinton was president in the 1990s. The players' immediate *lock-on* process, generated by these associations (hooks), made remembering plays easy. (The fact that they, themselves, choose the key *lock-on* words/phrases personalizes the process, thus making it even more effective.) This is just *one* application of analogy that Coach Lynch used with his players to help them learn what they had to know to play the game.

The Magic Connection

Think of all those hooks in that old school cloakroom; two rows of them. Each hook represents something for you; something or someone you know, a fact or set of facts that you know, an experience you had (good or bad) that made a lasting impression, a place that you've been, a favorite color, a favorite song, on and on. Each hook is *some thing* from your past, locked in your memory and unique to who you are. These are the personal things that happened in *your* life. They require no effort to remember. To use them, all you have to do is *think* of them. Maybe the so-strange way that your old Aunt Agnes eats a banana, smashing it into a pulpy mass before spooning it into her mouth, will be the hook upon which you will attach (associate) a new piece of information.

Now visualize that there are not just *two* rows of hooks, but *thousands, even millions* of hooks in your own cloakroom. And each one of them is a piece of knowledge or an experience, something that remains ever present in your memory! All you have to do is draw it up . . . remember it. It is a known entity, something upon which you can hang some new thing to be learned. By calling up one of your hooks, you can gain a new understanding that derives its meaning through its association or comparison with an old understanding, your *hook*. Learning something new is not such a daunting task if you *tie* the new thing to something you already know. As the previously referenced teenage girl might say, it's *like*.

Inside an Automobile Engine

If you wanted to teach a young boy about the internal combustion engine in your automobile and how it produces power to move the car, you might use a *hook* that he already had in his own personal *cloakroom*, one on which he could easily *hang* some new information. You know that the boy was at the Fourth of July celebration in town last week. He knows about the explosive power of firecrackers. Now show him an open can of tennis balls with all the balls removed except one. With the lid replaced on the can, this remaining ball can slide up and back. It bounces from one end of the can to the other and back again as the can is shaken. Now tell him to imagine what would happen if you took the ball out, quickly dropped a lighted firecracker into the can, and then quickly dropped the tennis ball back into the can, but did not replace the lid. What would happen to the tennis ball when the firecracker exploded? If not destroyed by the exploding firecracker, it would shoot out of the open can like a bullet!

By substituting an automobile's engine cylinder for the tennis ball can, a piston for the tennis ball, and exploding gasoline for the firecracker, the boy can see a relationship and grasp the analogy. With some further discussion, he can also be shown how the force of the piston moving inside the cylinder, if somehow transferred through a drivetrain to the automobile's wheels, would propel the automobile.

While there's a lot more to an engine's operation, you get the idea. Attach the new concept, the internal combustion process, to an already known concept, tennis ball fireworks! Now there exists a new *hook* for this boy, one on which something more may be attached in the future, say, learning how the pistons are attached to a crankshaft, the crankshaft to the driveshaft, the driveshaft to the differential, the differential to the axle, and the axle to the wheels.

If you wanted to get really silly but be *highly* effective, you might consider tying all these component parts into new lyrics for an old song, such as "Dem Dry Bones": "Toe bone connected to the foot bone, foot bone connected to the leg bone, leg bone connected to the knee bone . . ."[8]

By substituting the automobile parts in place of the bones, new song lyrics can be made up to sequence all of the parts, in order, of an automobile drivetrain. Once again, tying some new information (components of an automobile drivetrain) together via something already known (the lyrics to a song) is a powerful learning strategy, if a bit *wacky* at times. However, a *wacky* association generates a strong emotional response, resulting in stronger retention of new information. Wacky thinking is powerful thinking for learning/remembering!

Mom Always Said, "Pick Your Friends Carefully!"

Maybe your mother or father gave you this advice. When you were young and inexperienced in how people judge people, Mom knew that others were likely to judge her kids on the basis of who their friends were . . . by the company they were keeping.

Being judged by who your friends were back then may have seemed unfair to you, but it turns out that your mom was right. While *association* influences people in a societal context, association also has a substantial influence on how you learn. As shown by the automobile engine–tennis ball example, associating something you don't know with something that you already know is an excellent way to *hook onto* new information.

With this kind of association there does not have to be *any* relationship between the two things being associated: the new (unknown) thing and the old (known) thing. Just paste what you want to remember onto something you already know. The wackier the association the better! An example of this kind of MUC shows how helpful this can be even in learning definitions of new words.

A Large-Toothed Beaver and a World Religion

Ipana toothpaste was introduced in the 1920s and was the best-selling brand well into the 1950s and 1960s. A television advertisement in the 1950s featured a cute little beaver with large white teeth who danced across the black-and-white television screens of that time, advertising his favorite toothpaste, Ipana. More than a cute comic book character, Bucky Beaver was apparently successful in selling toothpaste. Bristol Meyers Corporation continued this brand until the late 1970s when it went off the market in the United States. It remains today the most popular brand in Turkey.

Bucky Beaver was known to all children in the 1950s, at least in households that had television sets. As TV was still relatively new at that time, not everyone had a set, but for those children who were able to watch television, they all knew Bucky! He was a celebrity! And strange as it may seem, that long-ago knowledge of a cartoon character advertising toothpaste on TV could be a big help to these children, now as senior citizens, in improving their vocabularies and learning new words. For example, Bucky could help them learn the word *Upanishads*, defined as the chief theological documents of ancient Hinduism.

Picture Bucky Beaver as a *Hindu* beaver! He is sitting in traditional Hindu clothing, legs crossed, in the *shade* of a tree. He is intently studying his religious book, the Upanishads. In this association, *Ipana* is a cue to think *Upana*, and Bucky sitting in the *shade* is the cue to complete the word *Upana . . . shad*. If this association seems inappropriate, even a bit sacrilegious, keep in mind that *because it is such*, it likely evokes the previously referenced *cringe response*. A helpful rule of thumb in forming associations is that the less politically correct way in which you learn something, the better you will remember it! Make it edgy, and you'll remember it well!

There is a *lot* of information packed into this beaver association, and while some may fall away over time (depending on how strongly you might choose to reinforce it at the start), it is likely that you will continue to remember *Upanishads* because of this Bucky Beaver association. You will not need to make a *conscious* effort to retain the association between Bucky and the word *Upanishads*. Once you form your initial association image, it will remain fixed firmly in your memory, even though you might wish otherwise! And if you are called upon to use this word often over time, you will find that the Bucky Beaver association is no longer needed because you will remember the word/definition just because of your frequent usage of it.

Cute and Funny Sticks!

Early 1950s to 1960s television broadcast a variety of advertisements that used cartoon characters to sell products. For those of you who watched television in those days, some of those most often aired will still be familiar: a tiny Santa Claus sliding down a snowy hillside on a unique sled (the triple heads of a Norelco electric razor); a cute little guy with a large white Alka-Seltzer cap; or Buster Brown and his dog Tige advertising shoes. Today's TV ads continue this strategy with animated M&M candy characters, an Energizer bunny, or a large white duck talking about insurance. All stimulate your visual, emotional, and physical senses, resulting in messages far more powerful and long lasting than just spoken-word descriptions of products.

Even when the selling of products relies upon words, even just *written* words, the people who write the advertisements take care in selecting their words carefully, choosing the ones they know will stimulate (pull) the physical, emotional, and visual *triggers* in you. Your response to these words may be under the radar of your conscious acknowledgment, but the words create an image in your mind nevertheless!

A Stick-Deodorant Tale

The makers of one underarm deodorant have captured the essence of Making Up Crap in the labeling of their product. Old Spice stick deodorant provides an example of how nonsense can help sell a product. On the back of the stick is written: "CONTAINS ODOR-FIGHTING 'ATOMIC ROBOTS' THAT 'SHOOT LASERS' AT YOUR STENCH MONSTERS AND REPLACES THEM WITH FRESH, CLEAN, MASCULINE 'SCENT ELVES.'" In the 1960s this same product had no such graphic labeling. A stick container of this era states: "24 hour deodorant protection."

As you well know, we live in a highly litigious society where lawsuits are filed at the drop of a hat, and yet no one has seen fit to file a false-advertising claim against the Old Spice people. This is likely because everyone knows that what is described on the product's label is just silliness, absurdity ... pure nonsense. It's *crap*! No attorney, even the hungriest one, would take a case alleging a charge of false advertising because the label descriptions are, to any reasonably intelligent person, all made up.

However silly, this form of labeling delivers a strong emotional, physical, and visual image to the customers as they decide whether or not they will purchase the product. Even though prospective buyers know that the statements do not reflect reality, their senses (emotional, physical, and visual) are stimulated by this form of messaging, inducing a greater likelihood that they will buy. The Old Spice people did not use nonsense language just to be funny or cute. This kind of language works!

Choose to Learn: *Do* Something!

Learning and remembering is accomplished when you *make a choice* to learn, and take specific steps to learn. Learning doesn't just magically happen, but happens as a result of what you do . . . what action you choose to take to *make* it happen. The most powerful action you can take is to attach your emotional, physical, and visual senses to that which you are trying to learn.

In his Tactics for Thinking learning process. Dr. Robert Marzano describes the value of our senses: "The attachment of mental pictures, emotions, and physical sensations to linguistic (word) descriptions of information is a powerful memory device."[9] It is clear that *how much* we remember of X, Y, Z is highly related *to how we learn* X, Y, and Z. Attaching emotion, physicality, and visual images to words generates a *retention grip* that is both initially powerful and long lasting.

English writer/philosopher G. K. Chesterton (1874–1936) was a master of analogy with a gift for conflating things that seemed to have no connection to each other. His statement about one's mind and mouth is an excellent example of MUC: "The object of opening the mind, as of opening the mouth, is to shut it again on something solid."[10] Chesterton's metaphor is relevant to Making Up Crap. If you wish to retain, remember, something that you put into your mind, it must be *solid* . . . memorable. Words are not nearly as memorable (solid) as your physical, visual, and emotional senses. So, wrap whatever you wish to remember in these three. Comingle the energy of each of these three, and become a synergistic thinker!

Synergistic Thinking = A Strategy Choice

Learning information is a function of how well you perform in four activities: taking information in, organizing it, storing it, and calling it up again. Enriching the information you wish to learn with visual, emotional, and physical properties makes that information something *solid*, something that you can hold on *to* in your memory banks. Using Chesterton's example, you should shut your mind on *solid* content, confident that it will be there when you want to get at it again. Synergistic Thinking *makes* that happen!

Synergistic Thinking is a process that captures *all* the elements necessary for you to become an effective and efficient learner. ST binds your emotions, physical sensations, and visual imagery abilities to the language (words) of what you are trying to learn. How these four thinking parts relate to each other is displayed in the "atomic structure" diagram of Synergistic Thinking (see figure 4.1). The core of the ST process, its atomic nucleus, is made up of *analogy* and *association*.

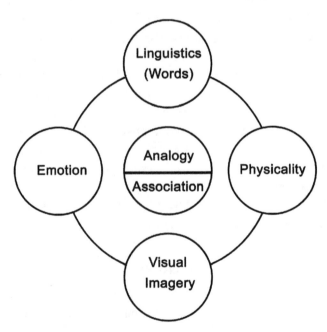

FIGURE 4.1. Synergistic Thinking "atomic structure"

Making Up Crap, Synergistic Thinking: What to Do and How to Do It

The product of *Super-Charged Learning* is *you* . . . becoming a more powerful and efficient learner. To get there, you apply a strategy, through a process, to get to a product. The strategy is Making Up Crap, the process is *Synergistic Thinking*, and the product is YOU . . . an empowered and powerful learner! Making Up Crap (the strategy) is accomplished by using your physical, emotional, and visual abilities (the process), which creates a powerful learner, YOU (the product). "Analogy and association," the nucleus of MUC's *atomic structure*, are what are used to make up the *crap*. But there is still more!

The Rest of the Story

A total-package *approach* to learning, the complete Synergistic Thinking atomic model, incorporates three more parts to the ST strategy: responsibility framing, concentration/focus control, and force of will. These three parts are explained in terms of how high-performing athletes, both university and professional, use them in their sports. There is a remarkable parallel between what athletes do to perform well and what students can do to learn well. The tools in both genres are the same!

Athletes may have somewhat of a learning advantage over nonathletes because their competitive natures are visual, physical, and emotional. Added to their well-accomplished skill sets in their respective sports, these three provide the *edge* that makes them successful. They are also, by their natures, focused, responsible, and driven to succeed. However, all human beings are innately visual, emotional, and physical beings, and becoming focused, responsible, and success driven can be learned. Chapter 7 brings it all together!

Notes

1. Andy Stanley, "The Comparison Trap: (Part 3), 'Two Bags Full,'" February 26, 2012, http://northpoint.org/messages/comparison-trap/two-bags-full.
2. Stanley, "The Comparison Trap."

3. Max Ehrmann, "Desiderata," 1927.

4. John McWhorter, *Doing Our Own Thing: The Degradation of Language and Music, and Why We Should, Like, Care* (New York: Gotham Books, 2003).

5. Dr. Charles Stanley, *Winning the War Within* (Nashville: Thomas Nelson, 2002), 19.

6. Miller Analogies Test, http://www.pearsonassessments.com/postsecondary education/graduate_admissions/mat.html.

7. Bill Lynch, former head football coach, Indiana University, 2007 to 2010, head football coach DePauw University, 2012, email from blynch@butler.edu to drgioman@q.com, Thursday, May 17, 2012.

8. James Weldon Johnson, "Dem Bones, Dry Bones, or Dem Dry Bones."

9. Robert J. Marzano and Daisy E. Arredondo, *Tactics for Thinking, Teacher's Manual* (Aurora, CO: Mid-Continent Regional Educational Laboratory, 1986), 15.

10. ThinkExist.com, G. K. Chesterton quotation, http://thinkexist.com/quotes/g._k._chesterton/4.html.

CHAPTER

5

Crappy Examples

NOW THAT you have a working knowledge of Making Up Crap, some real-life examples of what it looks like will help you see the possibilities this process has for you, and how you can tailor it to your own learning needs.

In the next few pages you will read about a large group of pachyderms (hippos) that was seen wandering onto a college campus. Even as you begin to read about this, you will know right away that it is a made-up story (crap); that it did not really happen. Only a small child might be taken in by such a tale, but your age-related knowledge of the-way-of-things allows for you to recognize nonsense when you see it. That's what makes nonsense/crap such an effective learning tool. As the late John Denver might say, it's *far out!*

A fundamental understanding of "learning" and "remembering" is important if you wish to try to do either. What is "learning," and what is "remembering"? Are they different from one another, or just the same thing with different word names? These are important questions. Once answered, the next topic will be much more entertaining . . . a *hippopotamus happening!*

Casual Acquaintances . . . or Close Friends?

For general purposes, learning and remembering are identical. To have *learned* something, some new piece of information, means that you *remember* it. For example, if you want to learn the parts of a flower (pistil, stamens, anthers, etc.), you will go through two steps: first, you will identify the names of these parts. Second, you will make an effort to remember the names that you have identified. You have learned this new information *only* if you are successful in *both* of these steps.

You find yourself in a biology class, and your teacher has just handed out a test. If the test asks you to identify the parts of a flower, you will be able to provide the correct answers: (1) if you were able to name these parts when you encountered them earlier, and (2) if you can remember them now. These two aspects of learning are *so* intertwined with one another so as to be almost indistinguishable from one another. You can think of *learning* and *remembering* as being the same thing. If these two were people, they would not be just casual acquaintances, but very close friends.

Brainy Stuff

Each of us has two limbic-system structures that allow us to form, organize, and store memories. Located on each side of the cerebral hemispheres, some people say they look like sea horses. They connect our emotions and sensory abilities (smell, taste, sound, etc.) to our memories, as well as act as memory organizers. They send memories out to the appropriate parts of the cerebral hemispheres for long-term storage, to be retrieved when needed.[1] The names of these structures are a combination of two Latin words, perhaps difficult to remember if learned by way of a stand-alone definition. But here's a *nonsensical* way to lock in the terms' definitions . . . using a humorously absurd story.

A Very Large Pachyderm

A older citizen drove back to visit his university alma mater, the place where he had so many wonderful experiences as an undergraduate student so many years earlier. It was a warm, late spring day. He had both driver-side and passenger-side windows open as he approached the beautiful campus where everything was still familiar to him after all the passing years. But as he was waiting at a stoplight at the entrance onto the campus, something began to happen that was completely unfamiliar to his past experiences!

While waiting for the light to turn green for his direction, he noticed that the cars that were crossing in front of him, having the green light, came to a sudden stop . . . while they still had a green light! At the same time, he began to hear a crunching noise from outside and behind the passenger-side window. It was the sound that you might hear while walking with leather-soled shoes on concrete on which gravel has been spread in the wintertime. As a late spring snow had fallen the day before, the streets still held some of this gravel.

The sound increased in volume, as whatever it was that was making it came nearer. The man arched his back and looked back over his right shoulder just in time to see a *huge* hippopotamus lumbering slowly past the passenger side of his car. As it went by he could smell the straw-dung, zoolike smell so characteristic of these animals. Behind this first one came a line of at least *ten to fifteen more*, all walking single file toward the campus entrance. All traffic was at a standstill, waiting for the line of animals to move past and onto the campus.

For a moment the man sat there in a state of stunned disbelief, wondering where these hippos were coming from and why they were walking onto *his* campus. Then it hit him! Of course . . . it all made *perfect* sense! He recalled from his undergraduate zoology class that the hippopotamus, like the elephant, is a member of an order of animals called *pachyderms*. These animals are highly intelligent and have outstanding memories. This was his clue. His university was a place of higher learning, a place where people went to learn, and remember. All of these animals were going there for that same purpose! His university was a "hippo-campus!" *Hippocampus* is the Latin-based name of the structure in the brain responsible for our memories.

It is not likely that you will *ever* forget the term *hippocampus*, or its function in remembering. You won't forget it because of *how you learned it*. You will remember the same way you remember the plot of a movie you saw, because it engaged you far beyond a linguistic (word) level.

Adults tell children stories by using words, but the children *remember* the stories through their visual, emotional, and physical talents. They use their sensory talents to create pictures of what happens in a story, and they attach to the story, subconsciously, the emotions and physical sensations that are taking place in them as they hear the story.

The child receives a story by means of words but remembers it through visual, emotional, and physical means. This how *everyone* remembers, learns. Linguistic pathways (words) are the means by which we *receive* information, but we *learn* information by using our physical, emotional, and visual abilities.

Young and old alike have the ability to remember stories of all kinds, and for the same reasons. Stories engage people's highly developed physical, emotional, and visual genomic capacities, our God-given human capacities that allow us to learn/remember better than any other creature on earth. The message: What you will remember about something, anything, is a function of how you took it in . . . how it came to you. If you can wrap new information in strong visual pictures, emotional reaction, and physical sensations, you will remember it strongly. You will *learn* it well!

Death, a Eulogy, and the Power of Story

Gary and Vince, close buddies since their high school days, were still the closest of friends as they went into their twilight years. Having gone through college together, they became teachers and taught in the same junior high school for their entire careers. They knew nearly everything about each other that there was to know, in some cases even more than their wives knew about them! Without warning, one was struck with a pulmonary disease that, after several difficult years, took his life. Along with so many of Gary's friends and colleagues, Vince attended the memorial service for his dear friend.

The minister who officiated at the service gave a wonderful talk about Gary, providing an enormous amount of detail about his life journey. What confused Vince, as he listened to the minister speak in such detail, was that he knew Gary did not attend church, nor did he have any close friends in the ministry. Still, it was clear that this man *had* to have been close to Gary and his family, for years, in order to know so much and to speak so authoritatively . . . without even the benefit of notes. Vince left the service perplexed.

Following the service, Vince found the answer to his quandary when he approached the minister and asked how he knew Gary so well. It turned out that the minister did not know either Gary or his family! He had been retained by the funeral director earlier in the week to deliver the memorial service eulogy. When Vince asked how he could *possibly* know all the intricate details that he referenced in his talk and relate them without written notes, the minister simply said that he had met with Gary's wife for an hour a few days earlier.

The minister told Vince that, during the meeting with Gary's wife, he had made some detailed notes. Later, he formed these details that he learned about Gary's life into a story, the story that he then told at the memorial service. His memorial story included the names of many of Gary's family members, his wife, their two children, their three grand-children, friends of the family, and many others. The four-number street address of the house where they lived as well as the length of time they lived there were included. Many more details of Gary's life were related, all in the precise order in which they took place during his lifetime . . . from birth until death. The minister told Vince that, in the week prior to Gary's service, he had delivered eight such talks.

Stories are powerful means of remembering because they are *super-charged* through the injection of emotions, physical sensations, and visual images of the people, places, and things in the story. Words are the medium for hearing a variety of facts, facts such as the minister heard from Gary's wife. Learning these facts, as the minster needed to do, occurs when the facts are tied together with physical, visual, and emotional properties . . . into a story. For this reason, a story is an excellent means of learning new information. The hippocampus story shows how to remember a word's meaning. But what the minister did shows how stories can be used to remember far more.

A Photograph Will Do Quite Nicely!

You may be thinking that, even though *story* may be an effective learning tool, it just takes *too* much time; words, words, words! But remember, you generate the story within your own mind. There are no *external* written or spoken words to intake and decode, just your mental conversation with yourself. This can take place with lightning speed compared to the time it takes to read about it here. But perhaps even this may seem to take too much time. But the storytelling process does not *stay* that way, a storytelling one! As you become more adept at using this strategy, what happens is that you begin leaving out most of the storyline telling and begin to see the entirety of the story in a snapshot, picturelike format.

Think of a film that you have seen, even one that you watched long ago. When the film's title arises in your mind, instantaneously you generate the essence of the film in your mind's eye. You do not go from scene to scene, but you have an instantaneous picture-clear awareness—characters, location, plot, action, ending, and more. You do not mentally identify each one by one, but they are all there. However, if asked to . . . you could do so. They are locked in your mind via this story-snapshot. This snapshot is strong in your mind's eye because it is *colored* with all of the physical, visual, and emotional ingredients that you experienced while watching the film.

What's more amazing is that you have to make no conscious effort to maintain a *lock* on these details. They will remain for years with no effort on your part. Wouldn't it be great to be able to lock onto your schoolwork material this way? A *nonsense* story strategy does this, bringing up facts and figures that you can remember almost as you can remember your favorite films. An example of such a snapshot story, one that you will *not* be able to forget, will seal the deal!

A Rich Guy, a River, and a Basketball Superstar

Here's another story, this one about a person's name, and remembering it in a way that you'd not be able to forget it . . . even if you wanted to! The man's name may be familiar to you . . . it is Richard Giordano.

The main character in this story is a *very* wealthy man! Now in his later years, he long ago disassociated himself from any avenues of gainful employment, simply because he had made enough in his early years to last a lifetime . . . several lifetimes actually. Having grown up in a typical Italian American family in the 1940s, his beginnings were humble indeed. But he is no longer of humble means, at least financially. Meeting him today, you would definitely refer to him as being monetarily "rich." (His nickname is "Rich.")

What is perhaps more interesting about this man, aside from his excessive wealth, is that he bears an *uncanny* resemblance to a world-renowned athlete. He is often mistaken for this athlete in airports around the world as he travels for his pleasure. In these instances, he has learned that it is far less trouble to provide the autographs that are requested than to try to explain that he is not the person he is thought to be. Another interesting coincidence is that this man's last name is synonymous with the name of a famous river—the River *Jordan*. In fact, the Italian word *Giordano* means "the River Jordan!"

You have probably figured out that the story's character, Richard Giordano, bears a striking resemblance to *Michael Jordan*, the former standout player for the Chicago Bulls. But what you probably don't know is that Michael Jordan is Italian! His last name was Giordano, but his managers convinced him to change it to Jordan when he entered the NBA because it would be more American sounding! The only difference in their respective physical appearances is that, unlike Michael Jordan, Richard Giordano is *old*! Thus the "O" at the end of the name Jordan.

Obviously, this story is almost entirely false! There is no way that a seventy-two-year-old Italian American looks *anything* like a young, black athlete! And, the assertion that Michael Jordan is Italian is just as absurd. Almost everything in the story is 100 percent fabricated nonsense! (The *only* factual part of this story is that the word *Giordano* actually *is* the Italian word for "the River Jordan.") However, absurd as this story is, it contains enough information, volatile information, to lock Richard Giordano's name in your memory banks. The information paints a picture of Richard Giordano with strong physical, emotional, and visual *snapshot* cues. Here are these snapshot cues as they are sequentially revealed in the story:

- Richard Giordano is a *very* wealthy person! He has so much wealth that he can be called "rich." ("Richard")
- His last name, Giordano, is actually the Italian word for the River Jordan.

- As everyone can see, he bears a *striking* resemblance to the famous NBA star . . . Michael Jordan.
- Michael Jordan's real name is Michael Giordano. He's Italian! He changed his name from Italian to English because his agent thought it would sell better in the American sports market.
- Although he looks like Michael Jordan, Richard is *older* than Michael. ("Giordan(O)")

The takeaway from this nonsensical story is that even hard-to-remember names can be learned/remembered if they are *colored* using the physical, visual, and emotional senses. Also, the absurdity of the physical association of an *old* Richard Giordano with a *young* Michael Jordan, race aside, makes for a *cringe effect*, further locking in the name association for the person hearing this story.

Going to the Bakery

Sometimes it may be helpful to have a preconstructed system to remember information, especially when the information comes to you as a list of items or things that are, or can be made to be, interrelated. Learning and remembering in these situations is made much easier as you use what is called a *rhyming peg-word* system. The following strategy can be called the *one-bun*, a list of sequential numbers that have a rhyming word associated with each.

1 – bun
2 – shoe
3 – tree
4 – door
5 – hive
6 – sticks
7 – heaven
8 – gate
9 – line
10 – hen

To use the one-bun strategy, first you must memorize this list of number-word associations. Rhyme is quite easy, so you will find that you can memorize this pattern in short order! Once you have locked this simple rhyming pattern into your memory, you are ready to apply it to a wide variety of learning situations. For example, a student in a beginning psychology class could use the *one-bun* to learn the ten subdivisions of psychology, information that might well show up on a future class quiz or exam. These are industrial, educational, personality, developmental, social, behavioral, health, sports, relational, and forensic.

The trick now is to form *strong* associations, those snapshot pictures previously discussed, between the key word (the word next to the number) and the subject matter (the subdivision itself). Infusing strong physical, emotional, and visual aspects makes the associations the strongest, and the most easy to remember. Keep in mind that there is actually *no order* for these subdivisions. (The #1 could be *any* of the subdivisions: behavioral, forensic, social, etc.) These ten subdivisions could be listed in any order if it would make associating easier for someone. Some examples will show how this can be done.

Industrial psychology might be an easy one to begin with. Perhaps you might think of the bun industry, and a large factory that turns out buns. You visualize buns moving along on a conveyor belt, on their way to a huge oven. You smell them baking and get a warm feeling at the same time. If you make these associations, it will be an easy task to call up "industrial" when you think "one-*bun*."

Number eight, sports psychology, is an easy association if you like to go to sporting events. You might think of the entry *gate* (eight – gate) that you have to pass through at a major sporting venue, like an NFL stadium. You might tie into the association the smells of the popcorn, taste of the beer, roar of the crowd . . . whatever you think of when you think of such a stadium. Making it *personal* makes the tie-in easy to remember!

One more: social psychology, number five, might be remembered easily if you associate the *social* nature of bees in a *hive* with the word *social* (five – hive). Again, you can tie in whatever emotion or physical sensations that might help you make this connection.

A Funny Thing Happened
on the Way to Remembering!

The one-*bun* rhyming scheme presented is not one that you *have* to use. You can choose different words to rhyme with the numbers, different from those presented here. For example, instead of "one-*bun*," you might like to establish "one-*sun*" for your system. It doesn't matter as long as you stick with what you initially chose. While the words presented herein are easy rhymes to remember for most people, feel free to substitute if you wish. Sometimes this can result in humorous outcomes!

Teaching this process to a group of university freshman football players, an instructor was surprised at how ingenious one of his students was. Subdivisions of psychology was not the topic in this class. The instructor selected a different topic because he knew that many of the players were taking an introductory business class as part of their freshman classload. In that class, the eight criteria required for a new business to be successful was what the students needed to remember. The first item on the list was that a business, if it hoped to be successful, had to have a *broad appeal to the general public*.

When it came time for the student-athletes to share what they came up with, the associations they used to remember these criteria, one player offered his association for number one, "a broad appeal to the public." He explained that he just thought of his girlfriend's *buns*, because he said that they certainly had *broad appeal*! Perhaps not politically correct, but effective! For this young man, the association he created had a powerful physical, emotional, and visual stimulus, so that he could easily remember the concept (broad appeal) through the word *bun*. This was a politically incorrect *cringe-effect* association, and a very effective one for him!

So What If You Can't Sing?

Whether or not you have any ability to sing, whistle, play an instrument, or even hum in tune, you likely appreciate music . . . some kind of music. And if you're like most people, there are certain songs that you can *play in your mind*, with the lyrics and melody as clear as the day you first heard them. For this reason, songs provide a terrific way of remembering lots of information, information that is completely unrelated to the songs whose lyrics are stuck in your memory. If you've ever been driving down the highway with a favorite song playing in your mind, you have the ability to use that *memory play* to learn new information. Knowing the words and melody are all you need!

A Long-Ago Rock and Roll Legend

The music of the mid to late 1950s was vastly different from what plays today. The songs of that era commonly told stories of love, conflict, life adventure, and more. The story lines unfolded for the listener through the combination of highly descriptive lyrics (words) and a pleasing melody (the music). Once again, a story is used to organize events.

To get an MUC learning result, the story of a song is important in that it arranges words, the words in the song, *in an exact sequence*. It is the words that, through the story line of the song, come to mind one after another, providing a ready-made paradigm for learning. These words are the hooks upon which new information can be attached . . . learned. A good example is found in a popular song of another generation.

Late at night in February of 1959, a plane crashed in an Iowa cornfield, killing all three passengers onboard. Killed were Buddy Holly, Richie Valens, and J. P. Richardson. Richardson was known as the Big Bopper. These three young men were wildly popular in the early days of the rock and roll era and were later immortalized in a song written by singer-songwriter Don McLean, "American Pie." Their music, individual styles, and personalities may be outdated in terms of music (or what *passes* for music) today, but the lyrics of one particular song of the Big Bopper, "Chantilly Lace," provides an example of how songs can be used in MUC.

In telling its story, "Chantilly Lace" uses words that are excellent for creating a learning frame . . . a framelike arrangement of hooks. Some of these words are *ponytail, pretty face, long-necked goose,* and more. In all, there are thirteen words arranged in the song's verse, and each word can be used as a hook on which you can hang/attach new informational items . . . thirteen of them!

Singing the U.S. Presidents

In a political science class, knowing who the presidents of the United States are would likely be something that would be expected of students. For example, the order in which the presidents held office might be an excellent test question. Knowing the thirteen words to "Chantilly Lace," in order as they appear in the verse of the song, is all that would be needed to remember these, at least the first thirteen.

For example, President Bill Clinton could be attached to the word *ponytail*, albeit in a highly politically incorrect way! Mr. Clinton's dalliances with members of the opposite sex could be seen as his *chasing ponytails*, or, more simply, chasing *tail*! Thus, when the word *ponytail* comes up in the verse of the song, Mr. Clinton comes to mind! In another politically incorrect association (to equally offend both major political parties), the name of President George Walker Bush might be similarly associated with *pretty face*, in that he did *not* have one! Once again, if you find these associations offensive . . . good! That's what makes them *stick* in your memory banks.

It should be clearly understood from these two examples that *edgy* association plays a big role in hanging new information on your memory hooks. The edgier the better! *Making Up Crap* makes use of your most wacky thinking, your bizarre side! Of course the song "Chantilly Lace" provides just thirteen memory hooks. But if necessary, you could remember all of the presidents, in order, by simply singing another song or two, in order, after "Chantilly Lace." And keep in mind that you make no effort at all in remembering your favorite songs, they are always there for you! Now consider the power of this process when used with the words of *rap music*! In many such "songs," the words themselves are edgy, certainly politically incorrect!

Getting from Here to There

A room in the house where you grew up is a *routing* framework. All children have powerful sensory memories. Everyone remembers the house or apartment where early years were lived. What was in each room and its location in the room is not forgotten. All you have to do is visually travel through your house, room to room, and each item in each room will come into view, in sequence as you go through your house.

For example, going through your living room, these items might come up as you go, from left to right: entryway, floor lamp, Dad's chair, sofa, coffee table, table at the front of the room, lamp on a table, television set, bookcase, and more. Each item, in sequence, gives you an object (hook) to which you can attach a new piece of information you are trying to learn. Here's a wacky association, if you were learning the bones of the human body. If you were at the part of the room where the table and lamp were, you might think: the *T-ibia* sound pronounces something like the *T* in *table*. Then, right next to the tibia in the lower leg is the fibula. Maybe you then associate the lamp with *F*-looding the room with its light.

In this scenario, the *table* appears in your mind's eye as you get to that part of the room, and the *T* sound brings to mind *tibia*. Then, as you move on to the lamp, you *see* it flooding the room with light, thus *fibula*. Wacky to be sure, and perhaps not the associations you'd come up with. But those you would make up would make sense to *you*! You would remember them strongly.

A route that you take each day as you travel to school, work, or to the grocery store can serve as a memory framework containing lots of hooks. In the same way that you went room to room in your house and identified objects as you went, you will identify things along the route as the hooks for this new memory framework. You might pass your neighbor's house, a fire station, the post office, and other easily recalled *things* as you visually travel your route. Each thing is an association hook on which you can hang/remember something. If you are studying anatomy, learning the sequential arrangement of bones in the body could be learned this way.

If you think of how many times in your daily life you go from here to there, you already have several ready-made memory frameworks to use, ones that already exist *in your mind's eye*! Just call them up and use them to learn new things. All that is necessary for this kind of learning is an easily accessible framework of hooks and your ability to think up wacky associations with which you tie new information to the known hooks, just as the names of presidents were *tied* to the words of "Chantilly Lace," or leg bones to living room furniture.

The Doctor Will See You Now

The field of medical practice is filled with wacky thinking! Not intended as an insult to the profession, young people studying to become physicians often find that wacky thinking is invaluable in learning information they must know. Scan the Internet for "medical mnemonics" and you will find sites in virtually *every* medical specialty. Doctors in training have developed and listed these over the years, and they remain in use across the entire medical community. The field of orthopedic surgery provides a good example of how wacky thinking in this genre functions.

Medical students who need to learn the skeletal anatomy of the wrist can use wacky-thinking frameworks. To remember the sequential order of the bones of the wrist, two somewhat politically incorrect paradigms might be used: "*Some Lovers Try Positions That They Cannot Handle,*" or "*Slowly Lower Tilly's Pants To The Curley Hairs.*"[2] Both provide a sequential naming of the bones of the wrist: Scaphoid-Lunate-Triquetrum-Pisiform-Trapezium-Trapezoid-Capitate-Hamate.

What is obvious in both of these is that there is an element of edgy or *colorful* language used in the paradigms—once again, the *cringe factor*. Causing an emotional response or physical recoil of some kind brings about stronger remembering, and medical mnemonic websites make good use of this rule. On the website referenced for these two examples alone, learning frameworks for *twenty-five* areas of medical science are listed, ranging from anatomy to genetics to neurology.

Another example, not as edgy, is used in the field of psychiatry. Those studying in psychiatry often use a simple system to learn some key evaluation-criteria categories. They lock onto the ten assessment criteria for evaluating a patient's state of mental health by simply remembering the name of a Japanese man, JIM MOTSIGA: *J*udgment, *I*ntellect, *M*emory, *M*ood, *O*rientation, *T*hinking patterns, *S*peech, *I*nsight, *G*rooming, *A*ffect.

Of course, there is a great amount of information resident within each of these ten evaluative categories, but learning and remembering the categories is the first step in the learning process. And like a medical student, you, too, can use similar wacky thinking systems to *easily* learn similar underpinning material that is necessary for what you do. Learning the basics is made far less arduous and time consuming, leaving more time for learning that is more intellectually challenging.

Whack-a-Doodle Science

Wacky thinking, while used often in higher-level medical sciences, is not often used enough by teachers in science classes in schools today. You may remember an elementary school science class in which the teacher told you about a fellow with a funny name, a name that helped you remember something about light and color: ROY G BIV. This guy with the odd name caused you to remember, as likely you do to this day, the full spectrum of the color of light as it passes through a glass prism: *R* = red, *O* = orange, *Y* = yellow, *G* = green, *B* = blue, *I* = indigo, *V* = violet. Add in ultraviolet if you wish to complete the *full* spectrum of light.

Astronomy is another area in science wherein you may recall something that you learned in early elementary school, if you had a wacky-thinking science teacher. This one has to do with learning the nine planets in our solar system, from the sun outward, by knowing something about a relative who baked pies. The mnemonic: *My Very Eager Mother Just Served Up Nine Pies. My* = Mercury, *Very* = Venus, *Eager* = Earth, *Mother* = Mars, *Just* = Jupiter, *Served* = Saturn, *Up* = Uranus, *Nine* = Neptune, *Pies* = Pluto. (Astronomers no longer regard Pluto as the ninth planet in our solar system, but as a *dwarf planet.*)

These wacky-thinking examples, some of which may still be used in science classes today, are rarely seen in subject matter outside of the science curriculum. Learning the U.S. presidents and the order in which they served is an example of how this approach can be used in a social studies curriculum. The hippopotamus story shows how vocabulary development can be stimulated in an English class. The one-bun is an example of learning in psychology. Almost *every* subject can be learned more strongly and efficiently through this wacky-thinking strategy . . . by *Making Up Crap!* Another example, this time in biology.

CHOPKINSCaFeMgNaCl

Some fifty-five years afterward, a piece of information that Mr. Maloney taught his sophomore biology class likely remains fixed in the minds of his students. The Chicago public schools were not highly regarded in the 1950s, but Mr. Maloney would have been titled "Top-Gun" in *any* school system of that time. The subject matter he was teaching the students in his sophomore biology class had to do with *photosynthesis*.

Photosynthesis is the chemical process wherein green plants take in sunlight and, through combining it with a variety of naturally occurring elements in the soil, make food (simple sugars) for the plant's growth and functioning. There are thirteen such elements required for this process to take place, so-called macro elements. (There are *trace elements* necessary, elements present in very small quantities, but these thirteen are the mainstays of the process.)

Mr. Maloney wove all thirteen into a simple short story about a short Italian guy who ran a restaurant. His restaurant was not famous for the food served, but for its salt! The Italian guy's name was Carmine, but everyone called him "C." Also, while he was definitely an Italian from the Old Country, he had an American name, "Hopkins." (Mr. Maloney offered no explanation for this anomaly.) The thirteen elements required for photosynthesis were wrapped up in this one-liner:

CHOPKINSCaFeMgNaCl

The phonetic reading is: "See Hopkins Café for mighty good salt!"

See	(C) calcium
H	(H) hydrogen
O	(O) oxygen
P	(P) phosphorous
K	(K) potassium
I	(I) iron
N	(N) nitrogen
S	(S) sulphur
café	(Ca) + (Fe) calcium-iron
mighty good	(Mg) magnesium
salt	(NaCl) salt

Mr. Maloney brought up something else that helped his students get a *picture* of "C." The south side of Chicago had a substantial Italian American population in the 1950s. Mr. Maloney took some time explaining that Carmine, the guy who owned the restaurant, was a little guy . . . not very tall, and that he was a frenetic, nervous sort of guy. "C," as he was called, was always running frantically about the restaurant, stumbling and knocking over chairs as he went, making sure that all the salt shakers were full!

Mr. Maloney even used a movie of the time that he suspected his students had seen, *Lady and the Tramp*. In this 1950s Walt Disney movie, there is a scene wherein the two main characters (dogs) are eating spaghetti at an Italian restaurant run by a short Italian man with a huge, black mustache. Since most of his students had seen the movie, Mr. Maloney led them to believe that this character was, in fact, "C"! A strong visual cue! These kinds of visual images, combined with carefully crafted physical and emotional components, served to keep learning for his students strong, over long periods of time.

Strange Stuff . . . Ooo-Eee-Ooo

A music-induced form of meditation using crystal bowls provides another means of wacky thinking. A compact disc, *Crystal Bowls Chakra Chants*, combines the calming tones produced by striking crystal bowls, with a mallet, with low-toned background chants.[3] If you don't happen to be a student of the Eastern religions, you may have no idea what "chakras" are. Chakras are anatomical location points on the human body, each of which has its own *color aura*.

Describing this medium to someone else would entail your knowing specifics about the auras, colors, and more. It would be helpful if you had an easy-to-remember grasp of the concept of chakras, colors, and more. A bit of wacky thinking can come in handy! The seven chakras, with aura color associations, are as follows:

CHAKRA NUMBER	LOCATION	FUNCTIONS CONTROLLED	COLOR OF AURA
7	crown	spiritual, control of all others, union with God	violet
6	third eye	mental, psychic, imagination	indigo
5	throat	communication	blue
4	heart	compassion and love	green
3	solar plexus	digestion, power, and mastery of self	yellow
2	below navel	sexual energy, reproduction, the life force	orange
1	base	elimination + related organs	red

Since each chakra has an ordinal position relative to the others (progressing downward from seven to one), the one-bun strategy is a good strategic fit for learning the sequence and location on the body of each:

7. The one-bun word here is *heaven*. As this is the top chakra, it is not difficult to envision a *crown* at the top of a human body. As it is the body part nearest *heaven*, it can be associated with the spiritual and God, and God *controls*.

6. The one-bun word here is *sticks*. A strong association might be to see a *third eye* in the middle of a forehead, a very sensitive mental eye. As this is the chakra, representing the mind via a third eye, everything enters through this eye and *sticks* in the mind.

5. In the one-bun, five is *hive*, and this is the communication chakra. As bees are quite active around their hive, furiously *communicating* with one another by making *throat* sounds, this is an easy association to make.

4. As four is *door* in the one-bun, it is easy to visualize the *heart* as the door to *compassion and love.*

3. The one-bun word is *tree.* As the *solar plexus*, the third chakra, is the area wherein the stomach is located, digestion is naturally associated with this area. If you have some knowledge of anatomy, you might envision a *tree* of vessels in the stomach . . . branching out. Through the digestion process, you gain *power and mastery of your actions.*

2. The one-bun word is *shoe*, and this one may be a bit of a challenge. The second chakra is located *below the navel*, and is associated with sexual energy, reproduction, and the life force. You know that the sexual organs are located below the navel; thus, you can associate *shoe* because shoe represents travel forward—a direction by which humans reproduce—creating *life force.*

1. *One = bun.* This is another easy association. The *base* chakra can be seen as one's *buns*, and a person's buns are at his or her bottom, or *base.* Elimination and organs related to the same tie in nicely in this visual.

These particular one-bun associations may seem cumbersome, tediously constructed, and, as a result, ineffective to you. There are two reasons for this: first, all of these are personal associations that are made by another person, not you! They are the result of someone else's wacky thinking, not yours! It would be unlikely indeed if another person would process this chakra information in the same way that you would.

Second, the mental associations explained here took an extraordinary amount of time, relative to the amount of time it took to form the associations. Such mental processing is usually *lightning fast*! This high-speed and highly personal phenomenology is represented in one final example of wacky-thinking learning, once again a highly *personalized* strategy. And remember, the very *first* association that comes into your mind will be the best and strongest! Don't try to think your way to better ones. Go with your first *instinctual* vision.

Bizarre Works!

There are memory championships, both in the United States and interna-
tionally, held every year. Joshua Foer detailed his experience in training
for and ultimately winning this competition in his book, *Moonwalking with Einstein*. He describes the contestants, a geeky crowd, showing up with blinders, earmuffs, earplugs, and a variety of paraphernalia
intended to block out all external sight and sound during the competition. Contestants must be 100 percent in their own minds, eliminating
all outside distractions.

Foer was given a deck of playing cards. His task was to learn
(remember) each card, in order, as he turned each card over to reveal its
face. To remember the cards, in order, he created a story wherein each
card he turned was a character in the story; thus, there were fifty-two
characters, one for each card in his story. In his book, Foer recounts
his storytelling scheme for remembering the first thirteen characters,
establishing their precise order of appearance and determining what
each represented:

> Dom DeLuise, celebrity fat man (and five of clubs) has been impli-
> cated in the following unseemly acts in my mind's eye: He has
> hocked a fat globule of spittle (nine of clubs) on Albert Einstein's
> white mane (three of diamonds) and delivered a devastating karate
> kick (five of spades) to the groin of Pope Benedict the 16th (six
> of diamonds). Michael Jackson (king of hearts) has engaged in
> behavior bizarre even for him. He has defecated (two of clubs) on
> a salmon burger (king of clubs) and captured his flatulence (queen
> of clubs) in a balloon (six of spades). Rhea Perlman, diminutive
> *Cheers* bartendress (and queen of spades) has been caught cavort-
> ing with the seven foot seven Sudanese basketball star Manute Bol
> (seven of clubs) in a highly explicit (and in this case, anatomically
> improbable) two-digit act of congress (three of clubs).[4]

Because the entertainment media labeled Michael Jackson the King
of Pop early in his career, you can understand the connection Foer made
between Jackson and the *king* of hearts playing card. However, most of

his other associations likely leave you wondering what's going on . . . in his head!

Prominent in many of his character constructions is the previously described *cringe factor*, the use of gritty and sometimes vulgar motifs used to lock onto information by eliciting the powers of emotion and physicality. However cringe-factor related his associations are, it is likely that Mr. Foer did not reveal to his readers the *exact* images he generated at the competition.

For example, he would not have generated the needed imagery power by thinking that Mr. Jackson had "defecated" on a salmon burger. Nor would the term "act of congress" come to his mind's eye in describing Ms. Perlman's activities with Mr. Bol. The more common *street* terms were more likely his choice. He probably used surrogates for these in his book so as not to offend his reading audience. But here, as in the chakra example, the uniquely *personal* choices he made work well for him, while possibly not for others.

There is but one criterion for effective wacky thinking in Making Up Crap, and it is simply *what works for the user*. This is the reason that *wacky thinking* is perhaps the *only* learning strategy whose utility is completely determined by and dependent upon the one using it. It matters not at all what someone else might choose to use, or how someone else's associations might be made.

As powerful a learning strategy as it is for individual learners, that characteristic is also the one that makes it difficult to teach. Along with its sometimes politically incorrect nature, its highly personal nature may account for why it is not often used by teachers in schools today. Wacky thinking truly takes a one-on-one individualistic teaching format, not a teaching-to-the-middle methodology.

Another reason for teachers choosing to refrain from using a Making Up Crap, and wacky thinking, approach in their teaching may have to do with social norms. As has been previously stated, the curse of political correctness has had a chilling effect upon freedom of expression in this country. The Speech Police seem to be everywhere in society today! With this cultural phenomenon in play, it is unlikely that teachers will choose to put themselves *out there* for the criticisms likely to come their way should they choose to use such unconventional teaching strategies as those associated with MUC. But thankfully, as a parent, you can choose to use these strategies in your home! You can keep those Speech Police out, and help your children learn with strategies your schools may be afraid to use.

Next, how athletes offer the very best example of a powerfully effective learning strategy: *Athlete-Powered Learning*!

Notes

1. "Hippocampus," About.com, http://biology.about.com/od/anatomy/p/hippocampus.htm.
2. "Anatomy Mnemonics," ValueMd.com, http://www.valuemd.com/anatomy.php.
3. Jonathan Goldman and Crystal Tones, "Crystal Bowls Chakra Chants," Spirit Music, P.O. Box 2240, Boulder, CO 80301.
4. Joshua Foer, *Moonwalking with Einstein* (New York: Penguin Press, 2011).

Education and Sports

ELPING PEOPLE, particularly young people, become well-informed and truly educated citizens is the goal of *Super-Charged Learning*. Elite athletes, full-ride scholarship athletes at universities, are super-charged learners in their sports. They also have something to teach about learning in general . . . away from the field of play! And it has to do with when learning *happens*. The "when" of learning is all important to these young people, and it is for anyone in a learning situation.

A brief look at teaching and coaching in today's culture is where the issue of *when* begins. Through what follows, you will see how it possible for elite athletes to achieve such high levels of sport performance. You will also see how you can do the same, achieving at similarly high levels of *academic* performance. You will be on your way to becoming an Athlete-Powered learner!

Teaching or Coaching?

If you *think about what you think* when you hear the word *teacher* compared to the word *coach*, part of what you come to probably includes some form of *status* difference between the two, a difference inferred by the definitions of the terms. Teacher: one who *teaches* or instructs, especially as a professional; instructor. Coach: a person who *trains* athletes for a contest[1] (emphasis added). Somehow, *training* seems to imply a lesser status than does *teaching*. Perhaps *training* is associated with trained animals, like a trained seal in a circus act. Teaching, on the other hand, may bring to mind a classroom wherein *cerebral* pursuits are choreographed by an educated person, a *teacher*.

Perhaps this characterization perception of being *trained* to dig a ditch as opposed to being *taught* to solve a quadratic equation is faulty in terms of the manner in which it assigns status to these activities. Both have practical value for those who are in need of their respective skill sets, but equation solving carries with it a higher status than ditch digging, likely because of its *cerebral* nature. Training seems to have a lesser status because it is largely viewed as a physical kind of activity, not a mental one.

It may be surprising to know that neurosurgery, a most highly esteemed cerebral endeavor, owes a large portion of its practice to training. Hardly the trained-seal scenario, but training nevertheless! The intensely intricate *physical* hand-eye-instrument manipulations of the neurosurgeon are trained. As any surgeon will tell you, these intricate physical manipulations are trained responses that are *coached* by those already proficient in these skills. Of course, surgeons are also highly educated via the large bodies of technical information they have to learn, all provided to them by *teachers*. It would seem that teachers and coaches have much in common, notwithstanding the different status society attributes to each.

There is no argument that team sports, both college and professional, occupy a prominent position in American culture. As a result, people who coach sports teams at both the college and professional levels are frequently featured in the media, their status in society being resultantly elevated. Media reports of the failings of public education have had the opposite effect upon the social status of teachers, their overall status declining. This media-driven story line helps feed the development of an almost contentious relationship between academics and sports in the public schools, one which makes it difficult for one to learn from the other.

No good end is served when a division between teachers and coaches exists within a given institution or nationally. Could teachers of subjects such as English, chemistry, or social studies learn something from football coaches? A closer look at each venue provides some answers.

Schools: Teaching

Educating children in this country has been anything but a static endeavor. Beginning in the early 1600s and progressing through four basic eras (permissive, encouraging, compulsory, and school choice),[2] the effectiveness of public education, and even its necessity, continue to be *hot* topics. The debate was refocused with the release of the early 1980s report *A Nation at Risk: The Imperative for Educational Reform*.[3] A committee of eighteen teachers, principals, superintendents, and college presidents issued its findings in 1983. They were *not* good!

Since the issuance of that report, public education has been under the microscope . . . an ongoing issue for public debate. A book, *A Place Called School* by John Goodlad, came out the following year, generating even more critical evaluation within university departments of education. While not specifically referencing the *Nation at Risk* report, Goodlad said, "American schools are in trouble. In fact, the problems of schooling are of such crippling proportions that many schools may not survive. It is possible that our entire public education system is near collapse."[4]

While published over *thirty* years ago, *A Nation at Risk* and Goodlad's assessment remain largely unaddressed in America's classrooms, while educators continue to debate the issues. The youth of the United States continue to perform poorly in test-result comparisons with other countries: South Korea, Finland, Singapore, Hong Kong, Shanghai, China, Canada, and others. Regarding recent comparisons, U.S. Secretary of Education Arne Duncan said, "This is an absolute wake-up call for America. The results are extraordinarily challenging to us and we have to deal with the brutal truth. We have to get much more serious about investing in education."[5]

From Mr. Duncan's statement, *staying awake* over time and remaining *serious* appear to be two things that teachers and administrators in the public schools have not been doing very well. Coaches of sports teams, by comparison, do not appear to be similarly challenged. They are very much both *awake* and *serious* regarding their duties. Their win-loss records tend to keep them that way.

Sports: Coaching

In drawing parallels between the coaches of successful university sports teams and teachers in the public schools, it is fair to say that there exists an existential difference in their respective clients. Public schools receive a broad range of clients (students) entering the process, in terms of their academic abilities; that is, students come with *all* levels of academic abilities, from the very high to the very low.

In comparison, university athletic departments receive a prese-lected group of clients (athletes) entering the process; for example, full-ride scholarship athletes, already highly skilled in their sports. The absence of a uniformly high scholastic ability of students entering the public schools contrasts starkly with the highly skilled athletes entering university sports programs. There is one area that stands out, more so perhaps than others, in comparing what teachers do and what coaches do. It has to do with the *time lines* in which they act on their clients, teachers with their students and coaches with their athletes. It is about seasons!

The Seasons of Our Lives

In America, as in all other cultures, lives are lived within a seasonal context. Virtually all of the things people do, week to week, month to month, and yearly, are done within an established time frame . . . a *seasonal* context. Everything is lived, done, and experienced within the context of its season, and once a season has passed, the activities of that season are not done again until its season arrives once again.

For example, all holidays take place in a seasonal framework. No one would think of putting up the family Christmas tree in July, nor would anyone likely go trick or treating in May. Every person has a life-clock fully wound up at birth and ticking onward until death. In between are all of the things done while living the seasons of experiences, year after year, and occurring in the same order. Perhaps King Solomon, in Ecclesiastes, said it best:

A Time for Everything

1 There is an appointed time for everything. And there is a time for every event under heaven—

2 A time to give birth and a time to die; A time to plant and a time to uproot what is planted.

3 A time to kill and a time to heal; A time to tear down and a time to build up.

4 A time to weep and a time to laugh; A time to mourn and a time to dance.

5 A time to throw stones and a time to gather stones; A time to embrace and a time to shun embracing.

6 A time to search and a time to give up as lost; A time to keep and a time to throw away.

7 A time to tear apart and a time to sew together; A time to be silent and a time to speak.

8 A time to love and a time to hate; A time for war and a time for peace.[6]

Seasons provide an organizational framework through which people organize their lives, living each day in an ordered and measured way and absent the chaos that would likely ensue in the absence of such an approach. For the most part, almost everything society does in this format works well over time, helping people live orderly, productive lives.

The one exception to the rule where this system does not serve people well, too often resulting in less than desired outcomes, is the way in which society educates its children. In education (schooling), the season approach has proven to be considerably ineffective. While the alternating seasons of sowing and reaping work well for farmers in producing crops, this arrangement has not been similarly productive for educating children.

It's Because of the Farmers?

If you ask anyone on the street why our public schools have lengthy summer vacations, you would likely get fairly uniform responses. Most people believe that our 1800s farming-based society is responsible for our current school-year calendars. The common thinking is that farmers needed to have their children on the family farm to help with the work during the summer months, and so schooling was suspended for this time period. However, it turns out that this conventional wisdom is not accurate.

In his book detailing the history of summer-school sessions in the United States, Kenneth Gold dispels the myth that an early farming-based society was the reason for the long public school summer vacations. Gold explains that summer sessions used to be an integral part of the public school calendar: "Summer's role was crucial to public schooling in the nineteenth century, when most young students attended and most female teachers taught during the summer. Urban and rural schools alike included summer terms, and most district schools were closed during the spring and autumn."[7]

With respect to agricultural needs, the closing of schools in the spring and autumn made more sense than closing them during the summer. Spring was the time for planting and the fall the time for harvesting, the times when farming was most labor intensive. Summers were merely the times when the crops grew to maturity, requiring far less need for labor in the fields. What we see in the demise of summer-school programs today had little to do with the needs of farmers but occurred largely as a result of other societal issues in play in the mid-1800s:

> Simply put, summer education is not widespread because of past ethnic and class fissions, conflicting beliefs about human physical and mental frailty, and processes of state growth and bureaucratic expansion. Political, ideological, and social forces pulled at summer from multiple directions, and historical actors brought a variety of agendas to bear upon it.[8]

The issues that led to the demise of summer sessions were many and varied. In city schools, summer sessions fell into disfavor partly because of the summer heat and the belief that young people could not be properly educated in hot city buildings. Budgetary crises, social pressures for extended vacations, political reform agendas, and other issues contributed to summer session declines in cities and across the country. There also existed a belief, expressed in the scientific/medical literature, books, and speeches of the time, that strenuous mental exertion during the summer might injure students, unless compensated by long periods of rest during the summer months.

A wide array of issues led to the demise of summer sessions, but agriculture's seasonal necessities played almost no role. Summer sessions in the public schools fell out of favor as a result of socio-political-economic influences. It was hardly the farmer's fault! The result was that in the mid-1800s, public education engaged a new approach to schooling and learning, an *off-season* approach. And for a similarly wide variety of socio-political-economic issues, our public schools continue in this format today. But is this mid-1800s-developed format working well for twenty-first-century children? Does it serve the needs of the children today? If the previously cited reports on American education are correct, the answer is a resounding NO!

Perhaps the guidelines for education would be more appropriate for the tasks at hand if they paralleled what is practiced in sports, wherein athletes, at least those serious about their performance abilities, observe no seasonal constraints for their activity. This may be the lesson that sports, more specifically those athletes playing sports, has to teach educators and society. It is this: there *are* seasons established for participation in sports, as well as stringent regulations governing participation. But the desire for excellent performance far transcends a seasonal approach.

Just a Little Sports History

The National Collegiate Athletic Association regulates more than four hundred thousand student-athletes, participating in twenty-three sports, at more than one thousand member institutions. In 1906, arising out of the need to protect student-athletes from abusive sport-related activities of the time (primarily on college football fields), then president Theodore Roosevelt summoned college leaders to the White House in an effort to put some protective rules in place. The result of this meeting was the formation of the Intercollegiate Athletic Association of the United States (IAAUS). In 1910 this organization evolved into the three divisions of the National Collegiate Athletic Association (NCAA) that governs intercollegiate athletics today.[9]

As was the case when the NCAA was founded, today's NCAA regulations protect the student-athlete from abuse and injury, but they have become equivalently important for the protection of the "student" aspect of the whole person . . . the "student-athlete." The *NCAA Division I Manual* (regulating large conference institutions) contains detailed regulations defining the quantities and natures of time that student-athletes may spend in their respective sports, both in and out of season.

For example, during the football season, a player's participation is limited to four hours per day, not to exceed twenty hours per week ("countable athletically related activities").[10] The out-of-season time when no contests are held has its own set of regulations for athletes' hours of participation, time off from prescribed athletic activity, class time missed, and more. Reading through this 426-page document is a reminder not only of the historically need-based foundations evident in 1906 but also of its necessity for protecting student-athletes in today's sports-oriented, media-driven society.

For student-athletes, the NCAA closely regulates *all* aspects of their university-related athletic activities. These regulations act largely on member institution athletic departments, administrations, coaches, and others to protect student-athletes from excessive infringement upon the time available for their academic pursuits. The regulations place limits upon how much time the institution and its agents may demand, both when the sport is being played and in its off season.

However, student-athletes may require more of themselves, and they do! The *member institutions* cannot make demands beyond NCAA proscriptions, but the student-athletes can and do, by choice, go well beyond these limitations. "Off season," for the committed student-athlete, is a nonexistent concept, NCAA standards and regulations notwithstanding.

While student-athletes from *all* sports continue a training routine in a year-round context, perhaps football players offer the most visible example of this ongoing engagement, irrespective of their sport being in or out of season.

Football Players, Excellence, and the "Off Season"

College athletics has become a year-round commitment. Student-athletes take advantage of every opportunity to develop their skills, watch film, and prepare their bodies for competition. There is no true off season from training. The competition is so great, that each athlete knows that they must continue to progress in order to compete at the most elite level. —Joe Scogin, PhD, associate athletic director, University of Tennessee

I believe a great majority of male and female college student-athletes want to WIN, and therefore feel compelled to commit to a year-round training regimen in their quest to be the best in their sport. —Charmelle Green, associate athletic director, senior woman administrator, Penn State University

In my experience working with Division I Football student-athletes, a large percentage of these young men view their involvement in organized athletics as more than extracurricular. The year-round commitment to developing themselves both physically as "students of the game" more closely resembles a professional honing his craft. At their core, even more influential than lofty professional aspirations, exists an identity often defined by success on the field. This dynamic, combined with ample perks inherent to their social status, can drive young men to embrace a consuming training regimen. —Adam Sargent, associate director, academic services for student-athletes, University of Notre Dame

The evolution of collegiate athletics has essentially pushed student-athletes to maintain a level of dedication so much further beyond what many think of when they analyze what it means to be a collegiate athlete. Due to the time demands from the athletic side and the pressures to succeed, year-round training is necessary to be productive at a high level. This is not isolated to revenue sports, rather the Olympic sports are also in a competitive environment that forces student-athletes to work on their craft throughout the year. Those who are the most successful understand this concept and quickly realize the level of adjustment that needs to be made on this level if they are to distinguish themselves. —Kimya Massey, director, academic services for student-athletes, University of Central Florida

In addition to the coaching staff, a cadre of SASS (Student-Athlete Support Services) staff, such as those cited above, maintain a twelve-month contact and communication with layers. This group of learning specialists and academic counselors/advisors helps players balance the rigors of their sport involvement with their academic responsibilities. And while players only *formally* practice their sport within a seasonal context, adhering to NCAA standards, SASS staff remain connected with them in a three-phase framework: during the football season in the fall, during the remainder of the school term once the football season is ended, and during the summertime.

Nearly *all* football players (on Division I squads) remain on campus during the summer term to continue their athletic training. Many also continue their academic studies during this time as well. For *both* players and their SASS staff, there is no such thing as *off season*.

As is apparent, football players as well as other university sports participants are diligent in their pursuit of athletic excellence. They know that their success would be substantially curtailed if they worked at their sport within a seasonal context. Effective learning, *Super-Charging Leaning*, makes the same judgment. Like elite athletes, elite learners must address their educational goals and aspirations in a non-seasonal format. Even though a normal K–12 school year may end as summer begins, learning must continue if excellence is truly a goal. This is *Athlete-Powered Learning*. This is where parents come in to play a very important role!

Notes

1. *The American College Dictionary* (New York: Random House, 1966), 573.
2. "A Brief History of Education in America," Clare Boothe Luce Policy Institute, http://www.cblpi.org/ftp/School%20Choice/EdHistory.pdf.
3. *A Nation at Risk: The Imperative for Educational Reform*, A Report to the Nation and the Secretary of Education, United States Department of Education, by the National Commission on Excellence in Education, April 1983.
4. John Goodlad, *A Place Called School* (New York: McGraw-Hill, 1984), 1.
5. "In Ranking, U.S. Students Trail Global Leaders," USAToday.com, http://usa today30.usatoday.com/news/education/2010-12-07-us-students-international -ranking_N.htm.
6. Holy Bible, Ecclesiastes 3:2–8, New American Standard Edition, 804.
7. Kenneth Gold, *School's In: The History of Summer Education in American Public Schools* (New York: Peter Lang, 2002), 1.
8. Gold, *School's In*, 2.
9. Rodney K. Smith, "A Brief History of the National Collegiate Athletic Association's Role in Regulating Intercollegiate Athletics," *Marquette Sports Law Review* 11, no. 1 (Fall 2000), http://scholarship.law.marquette.edu/cgi/view content.cgi?article=1393&context=sportslaw.
10. *NCAA Division I Manual, 2011–2012*, Rule 17.1.6, "Daily and Weekly Hour Limitations—Playing Season," 2138.

Athlete-Powered Learning

A THLETES HAVE been described as having three extraordinarily well-developed abilities: visual, emotional, and physical. And while these live large in generating excellence in athletic performance on their respective fields of play, they also are critical to learning in their academic pursuits, their university academic classes.

There are three additional abilities that athletes have developed that make them successful in their sports: the abilities to focus tightly without distraction, to take 100 percent responsibility for outcomes, and to pursue goals with a strong force of will. These, along with their visual, emotional, and physical abilities, form the totality of Athlete-Powered Learning. Combined with a Synergistic Thinking learning strategy, they apply efforts in their learning and performing venues that make them the star performers that we see!

This kind of learning, Athlete-Powered Learning, is available to everyone! What follows will show you how you can apply these abilities to every learning challenge that comes your way and come out a winner on your *academic* field of play!

Going to the Picture Show

Motion pictures are often just a diversion from daily reality, a source of mindless entertainment. However, on some rare occasions they offer valuable insights into how we live and how we might live better. Two older movies with quite different story lines are examples of this: 1985's *Out of Africa* and 1990's *Hard to Kill*.

In a scene from *Out of Africa*, Denys Finch Hatton (played by Robert Redford) is having an intimate conversation on the African grasslands with his paramour, Karen Blixen (played by Meryl Streep). As they sit on the grass, Karen voices her objections to Denys's behavior in their relationship: how he frequently goes off on extended hunting trips, his friendship with another woman, and his lack of commitment to her. She suggests that he should change. He responds: "I don't want to live someone else's idea of how to live. Don't ask me to do that. I don't want to find out one day that I'm at the end of someone else's life."[1]

In *Hard to Kill*, Mason Storm (played by Steven Seagal) is having a conversation with his friend and ally Lt. Kevin O'Malley (played by the late Frederick Coffin). Things have not been going well for the two of them as they battle the bad guys and they find themselves in difficult straits. However, with strident assuredness, Storm says to O'Malley: "We're outgunned, and undermanned. But you know sumpin'? We're gonna win. And I'll tell you why. *Superior attitude. Superior state of mind*"[2] (emphasis added).

The wisdom in these lines of dialogue might easily escape most of us as the plot moves quickly on to the next scene. They are *just* movie lines intended to entertain. But taken together, these two sets of mere movie dialogue portray the fundamental belief systems upon which successful athletes establish and build their successes. They are the bedrock of a central characteristic of Athlete-Powered Learning . . . a powerful *force of will*!

Education Alone . . . No Sale!

It is unlikely that anyone in America today would be uninformed about the health dangers resident in being overweight or of being a smoker. Everyone should be well educated about these topics. However, notwithstanding an abundance of education, over 17 percent of Americans still smoke.[3] Data on obesity are not any more encouraging: "More than one-third of U.S. adults (35.7%) and approximately 17% (or 12.5 million) of children and adolescents aged 2–19 years are obese."[4]

So how can it be that so many people, well educated regarding the health risks, still choose to smoke and/or be fat? The important word here is *choose*! These people *choose* to smoke and/or be fat. They refuse to choose *not* to smoke and/or be thin. People can *make a decision* to quit smoking and maintain a healthy body weight, but they do not exert the *force of will* to make the behavioral change required to accomplish the result. Being educated is not the issue! Desire to act is not the issue! Generating and sustaining a disciplined *force of will* to achieve a result is the issue. In his May 2013 sermon on his weekly television program, Dr. Charles Stanley stated it succinctly: "It is discipline not desire that determines your destiny."[5]

Some people say that *education* is the answer for the societal problems that plague us. However, like smoking or being overweight, education is a choice, a decision one must make. Choosing *not* to be educated is the direct route to ignorance, and stupidity may come along for the ride. The late John Wayne had his own unique way of stating the obvious: "Life is tough, but it's tougher when you're stupid."[6] Like living stupid, living ignorant is also tough. But knowing on its own is not enough. You have to *act* on what you know!

A School Principal's Fiasco

Suspensions from school failing to produce a very good result, a high school principal decided to address the student smoking problem at his school in a way that emphasized an *educational* approach first. He thought that punitive measures should be just a second resort, a way to address students' failure to act if education did not work. He obtained booklets from the American Cancer Society that explained, in clearly understandable terms, the negative effects of smoking on the human body. The pamphlets provided simple statistics on the health risks associated with smoking (death rates, organ damage, etc.), effects of quitting, and some hints on how to stop smoking.

Using this information, he made up a ten-question test. Students who were apprehended for violating the school smoking rules were given a choice as to the nature of their punishment: (1) they could choose the traditional three-day suspension; or (2) they could choose to take the test. If a student chose the test, he or she was provided a pamphlet to study, after which the test would be administered.

If the student passed the test with 90 percent accuracy, answering nine out of the ten questions correctly, no suspension would be required. If the student missed more than one item, an additional study period would be allowed after which a slightly altered test would be administered. If the student still missed more than one item, a one-day suspension would be assessed. There was one additional requirement in the process, and that was that the student's parents had to give their approval for the option their son or daughter had selected. And here is where the difficulty arose!

In addition to sending the student home with the pamphlet from the American Cancer Society, the principal required the student to return a parental consent form. This needed to be signed, by the parent, for the process to go forward. The consent form contained a few paragraphs about smoking and those who smoked. It distinguished between those who were not informed (educated) about the dangers of smoking and those who knew but smoked anyway.

People in the first group, those not aware of the dangers of smoking, were termed "ignorant" but capable of being educated . . . the focus of the pamphlet. People in the second group, those who knew the dangers but smoked anyway, were termed "stupid." Knowing that something would hurt you, but doing it anyway, was the criterion for the "stupid" label.

The result of parents reading about the two groups described in the principal's consent form was unexpected . . . but understandable. The principal received a *great* deal of blowback from many parents, with a variety of confused comments about what he was requiring of *their* children. What the principal had not factored into his plan was that many of the parents would likely be smokers themselves. They did not take kindly to being labeled as "stupid," especially in front of their children! So much for this principal's *educational* approach! While academically accurate, it turned out to be a bit too direct, if not politically incorrect, at least for some parents.

Education, like most things in life, is a choice. As the Nike advertisement says, *Just Do It!* All that education can do is to *show* a range of choices and the relative validity of each. *Choosing* is perhaps the real answer. To make the really hard choices, *force of will* is a necessity! And as in the case with the parents described here, some realistic self-assessment and humility might also be helpful!

Force of Will: The Necessary Ingredient

Perhaps there is no better characterization of force of will than the life of Dr. Charles Krauthammer. Dr. Charles Krauthammer is a regular on Brett Baeir's *Special Report* program each evening on the Fox News Channel. On October 25, 2014, Baeir hosted a one-hour special program in which the life of Dr. Krauthammer was presented. As many know, Dr. Krauthammer is paralyzed as a result of a diving accident when he was in his early twenties and has been in a wheelchair ever since.

At the time of his life-changing accident, Dr. Krauthammer was a medical student at Harvard University. Still in the hospital following the event that took away his mobility, he immediately arranged for his studies to continue via special visits from his professors and some assistance in placing books before him so that he could keep up with his assignments. He did not wait even a moment to resume his direction in life, to become a medical doctor. Baier tells us how it turned out: "With such *force of will*, Krauthammer graduated on time in 1975, and near the top of his class"[7] (emphasis added).

Athletes have no deficits in the force of will department! If there is one defining characteristic of high-performing athletes, it is that peak performance is determined not *just* by God-given talent or highly tuned skill sets but by force of will. This does not imply that athletes are born with a dominant force of will gene or that their attitudes for task accomplishment are inbred. Attitudes, like other behavioral traits, are learned responses to circumstances—they are developed. Performance psychologist Dr. Jim Loehr, cofounder of the Human Performance

Institute in Orlando, Florida, speaks to attitude and what constitutes *peak* performance:

> For as long as sport has been enjoyed, coaches have told their athletes to develop a "good attitude." As the coaches' saying goes, "Attitudes are the stuff of which champions are made. When teams have negative attitudes, they don't play well and they don't win.
> *"With the enthusiasm that accompanies a positive attitude, everything else becomes possible."*[8] (emphasis added)

Football players, for example, know that their skill sets may be on a par with those of their opponents on any given afternoon. What then will determine victory?

> An Ideal Performance State (IPS) exists for every athlete. It's simply the optimal state of physiological and psychological arousal for performing at your peak. Arousal is reflected in heart rate, muscle tension, brain wave frequency, blood pressure, and a host of other measures. IPS is typically accompanied by a highly distinctive pattern of feelings and emotions—a most fascinating discovery. You are most likely to experience IPS and perform at your peak when you feel: Confident, Relaxed and calm, Energized with positive emotion, Challenged, Focused and alert, Automatic and instinctive, Ready for fun and enjoyment.[9]

To the extent that these learned responses are in place at game time, precipitating the presence of an Ideal Performance State, an athlete's potential for winning is at its peak. What this means is that all the God-given talent, combined with the skills development by the athlete, will be maximized at a 100 percent level, with nothing *left in the locker room.* This ability of an athlete to *volitionally* (choose to) bring about a positive attitude at game time is an example of the human genomic trait referenced in the subcategory Volition and Superiority discussed in chapter 2.

The athlete can *make it happen.* He determines his emotional state, attitude, and mind-set through his own force of will. Similarly, the athlete can (as can anyone!) *volitionally* choose an attitude toward academics, as well as choose to engage a Making Up Crap strategy for learning academic subject material. This is *force of will* in the atomic structure paradigm of Synergistic Thinking (see figure 7.1). Force of will places the *person* in charge of outcomes while not allowing existent circumstances to dictate anything else!

Joel Osteen, pastor of the Lakewood Church in Houston, Texas, states this principle in a broader and far more pervasive life venue: "Happiness does not depend on your circumstances; it depends on your will. It is a choice that you make."[10]

The Dog Ate My Homework!

A funny one-liner offered to his teacher by a child who failed to complete his assignment, this response to personal failure is *not* part of an athlete's

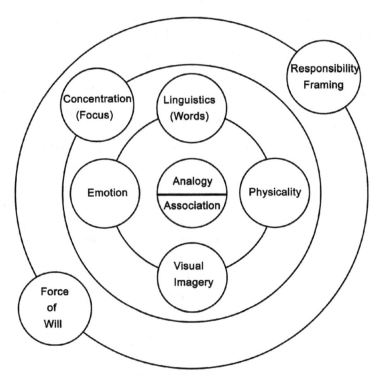

FIGURE 7.1. Synergistic Thinking "atomic structure"

repertoire. All successful athletes have a common understanding about what determines their performance on the field of play. It is them!

This understanding is exemplified by Tom Spasoff, a competitive swimmer at the University of Illinois in the 1960s. As part of his training regimen, Tom had to do hundreds of pool lengths of kicks, using his kickboard. For those not familiar with this kickboard training activity, a swimmer uses a flat, usually Styrofoam, board, extended forward at arm's length, and propels through the water with just the power of leg kicks. Tom had printed "NO ONE BUT YOU!" on the top side of his kickboard in large, black letters. This motto was ever present in his sight at times when his practice sessions were the most difficult. He knew that success as a Big-Ten swimmer was not going to come through anyone's efforts but his own. It was *all* up to him! "The dog ate my homework!" excuse would not work!

This single-dimensional view of training and success, common to successful collegiate athletes, is what is termed *responsibility framing* in the Synergistic Thinking atomic model. It is the window through which athletes view their participation in their sports, not only their training but also their on-field play. *No* football player who played his position poorly during a series of downs comes off the field believing that his performance was the result of any other person but himself. Nor does his coach! When an athlete looks at the *responsibility frame* for his performance, he sees but one image framed therein . . . himself!

The late General Norman Schwarzkopf said it succinctly: "When placed in a position of command, take charge."[11] Athletes have to take charge of their studies as they take charge of their position play on the field, with a "no one but you" frame around their actions. The goal of *Super-Charged Learning* has this same focus. *Take charge* of your studies by taking a strategic action. As it is with athletes, the *responsibility frame* contains only one picture . . . you! Powerful minds, in addition to powerful bodies, result from this can-do/must-do attitude.

Do I Need Glasses/Contacts?

For those who have worn corrective lenses for any length of time, either eyeglasses or contact lenses, an understanding of why we could not see clearly without these is understood. The reason for impaired vision is that light rays focus at a point behind the retina or in front of it, but not directly on it. The result of this deficiency of focus is a blurry image due to a lack of focus. Corrective lenses force the light rays to target dead center on the retina, providing a cleared-up picture once again.

Many people, without respect to age, experience a similar *psychological* phenomenon when they try to read a page or listen to a lecture. The mind wanders, focus diminishes, attentiveness becomes blurry, and it is said that the person is not "paying attention." The most important word, and most often overlooked, in *paying attention* is *paying*. You need to *pay*! Dr. Majid Fotuhi explains how critical paying attention is:

> Paying attention is the single most important practice for attaining better memory skills. Attention is the process by which you focus all of your senses on one issue. The more you pay attention, the more likely it is that the information you want to remember will be firmly *registered* in your hippocampus.[12] (emphasis added)
>
> For you to remember something you read or to recall someone's name, you first need to *register* that information in your brain (and especially in your hippocampus) clearly and firmly. Then you need to retrieve that information. For this to happen, you need to be mentally alert, awake, and interested. This may sound obvious, but in fact most people don't appreciate it.[13] (emphasis added)

There are four primary steps in learning any new information: taking it in, organizing it, filing it, and calling it up again. The *taking it in* is the "registration" part, encoding and entering it into the hippocampus. In a computer analogy, the hippocampus is your RAM, random access memory. Its job is to *identify* information (register it), and then shuttle it out for permanent storage in the cerebral cortex, your intellectual *hard drive*. If something does not make its way into the hippocampus for processing, it cannot be sent out for storage in the cerebral cortex.

If you do not pay close attention when you first encounter new information, it is a good bet that it will not be formatted completely enough for it to register in the hippocampus. If that happens, the information cannot be passed on into the cerebral cortex and will resultantly be forgotten. *Paying* close attention is critical!

You Want to Buy . . . You *Must* Pay!

When you purchase an item, say groceries from the supermarket, it is well understood that you have to give something up (money) to obtain the groceries. The store management likely will not take kindly to your walking out with groceries without paying for them. It's called theft! In a word, you are not allowed to get something for nothing.

It's no different with *paying* attention. You don't get something for nothing here either. In order to obtain information from a lecture, understand a textbook assignment, or have a meaningful interaction with another person, you have to *pay*, give away, something. What you have to *give away* is anything that gets in the way of you getting the information . . . from the lecture, book, or conversation. You have to mentally set aside everything else. You have to give up these distractive thoughts . . . *pay* them away.

Perhaps you have always believed that you are unable to pay attention as other people are able to do, that it's just part of your nature and that you can't change nature! However, it may be more about *you* not taking responsibility! But it's not all that difficult to change that situation. There are real and tangible ways that *you* can increase your ability to pay attention. You need not be held hostage to outcomes that are the result of a directionless and wandering mental state.

Just as putting on corrective lenses is a strategy (an action one takes) for sharpening the focus of eyesight, there are strategies (actions) that can be *put on* to sharpen your focus for gaining information . . . learning. The fact is that everyone suffers from loss of focus (not paying attention), and everyone can benefit by putting on these corrective lenses (strategies for focus) to get the information they need.

Athletes have developed the capacity to focus perhaps better than most. A football player on the field during a game often does not hear the crowd noise. And it is not that they have some natural ability to focus, but that they have sharpened their focusing abilities over time, through purposeful practice. Athlete-Powered Learning is reliant on a first important step, a tight focus. But how do you get one?

Good Diagnosis and the Right Prescription

A tactical approach to paying attention relies upon introspection, both initial and then ongoing, throughout the time period in which paying attention is needed. Specific questions require answers: (1) To what, *specifically*, do you need to give your attention? (2) What is your energy level? Are you anticipating, energized, and focused, or are you tentative, weak, and distracted? (3) With questions 1 and 2 answered, what tactics can you engage to maximize your attention-payment status? This is the *diagnosis* part, and it is important!

While it may seem silly to be asking such basic questions, doing any job correctly always requires some up-front analysis, followed by the selection of the right tools for the job. Finding out *why* your car is running poorly prefaces taking any action you might take to fix it. Installing a new battery in your car would be a feeble attempt at repair if the problem responsible for its not running is a malfunctioning fuel pump.

Put It Away, *Somewhere* . . . Now!

Determining the object to which you need to pay attention is usually the easiest part. Let's say that you are entering a classroom wherein you will be hearing a lecture on zoology. One problem for you is that there are lots of other people entering this classroom, and some are highly attractive members of the opposite sex. You've been busy with football practice as well as the homecoming game this weekend and haven't had any time for dating. Needless to say, the main attention-getter in this crowd, for you, is not likely to be the professor at the front of the room discussing the taxonomy of phylum Porifera, sponges!

As you enter the classroom, it is of foremost importance that you *decide* that the professor is going to be the focus of your attention, sponge-related boredom aside. Doing this may seem silly, but the body follows the directions of the mind, so you need to get your *whole self* moving in the right direction at the outset. If you have made the choice to attend to the professor and not the person of the opposite sex in the next row, good choice! However, an initial choice of this kind in no way insulates you from mentally wandering off course, back to that other person . . . or a variety of other things. So keep your decision foremost in your conscious mind!

Maybe you're having financial problems, your car needs repairs, or you're thinking of the player who will be your opponent, playing the position opposite you in the upcoming game. A wandering mind is normal, but you *can* affect how much wandering goes on if you choose to use some simple strategies.

Time to Build Some Brackets

If you have a variety of issues that are weaving their way into your thoughts as you try to pay attention to something, *bracketing* is a useful strategy that will allow you to focus on what's important. Bracketing is a process wherein you deposit the distracting items in a safe place, a nondistracting place that is away from you. Using your visual-physical-emotional abilities is all that is necessary to bracket interfering thoughts.

Visualizing a very large roll-top desk is a good image-place to begin. It will be your repository for all the things that are distracting you. If you picture a roll-top desk, you see several little drawers along the top of the desk, extending across the top from one side to the other. Picture yourself opening these little drawers, one by one. Into each drawer you deposit a distracting issue, one per drawer, and close it, until all your distractions are closed securely into these drawers. Feel the absence of these from your mind as each distraction is deposited! You are now ready to focus on what requires your attention.

The roll-top desk is just one of many visual images you can devise for a bracketing strategy. What's important is that you define some *physical* places to put your distractive thoughts. Perhaps a multitiered jewelry box, lockers in the gym, or rows of post office boxes will work for you. For bracketing to be effective, all you need to do is *see and feel* the places where you will place your distractive thoughts . . . and then deposit them there!

As effective a tactic as it is, bracketing strategies may not work over long periods of time, and distracting thoughts may return. In the case of reading a textbook, you may find that you've read through two complete paragraphs only to realize that you have no idea what was read! It's like driving down the highway on a long trip, knowing that you have been a careful driver but having no recollection of the scenery that you have passed by in the last half-hour.

Being aware of your state of attention is the first step in paying attention! Attention and focus can slip away from you almost unnoticed. The trick is to catch the *slip away* early so that you can take action to make a correction . . . before too much of a chapter, lecture, or whatever the activity gets past you. When you *sense* that you have wandered off track, an immediate *payment* must be made, payment resulting in a return to focus. You have to pay (give away) the distractive element immediately, so that it does not continue to interfere with your focus.

Say It Away!

A movie that was not a large box office success had a strong message about force of will and winning. *For Love of the Game*[14] starred Kevin Costner as an aging baseball pitcher in the twilight of his career and pitching his final game for the Detroit Tigers.

Near the end of the film, he is on the mound and working on a no-hitter. With the fans against him and loudly hurling insults as he stands ready to deliver a pitch, Costner's character, Billy Chapel, struggles to gain control of his emotions. The camera zooms in for a tight shot of Chapel's face. At this point, the film directors take viewers inside Chapel's mind, to hear what he is thinking as he thinks about his predicament.

Looking into Chapel's eyes, viewers hear him *think*: "Clear the mechanism." At once the incredible roar coming from the fans in the stands diminishes to a nearly inaudible level. He no longer hears the fans! Their noise has been relegated to a nonissue for him as he pursues his job of pitching to the batter in front of him.

"Clear the mechanism" is an example of a concept called *affirmation* (self-talk), a mental-toughness strategy taught and coached in athletics. It is a way of talking to yourself and telling yourself that the outcome you desire is, in fact, already in place. It is a highly personalized emotional-psychological strategy that athletes use to gain control and balance when, like Billy Chapel, "all hell is breaking out" around them.

In the film, Chapel centers on a simple three-word phrase to calm, organize, and focus his thoughts. In Chapel's mind, hearing these self-recited words transports him to a place where the fans cannot reach him. He closes the door on the crowd, shuts them out of his hearing. This is largely the same strategic action that allows football players, in a stadium filled with thousands of cheering fans, to hear *none* of it. It is the same strategy that you can use, a "say it away" tactic, to block out thoughts that are getting in the way of your focus.

The Best Way?

There is no *one* best way to get rid of distraction that works with uniform results for everyone. The best one for you is the one that *you* devise, practice, and develop. Your ability to focus your attention on any one thing is tied up with who you are and how you operate. That's why the examples of MUC that were described earlier might or might not work for you. They are not *yours* . . . *you* did not create them!

Like made-up *crap*, what works for you in focusing your attention is what is best for *you*. *You* are the architect of the best tactics for *you*. The key is coming up with your own visual device/place, and then empowering it with your emotion and mentally constructed physical actions.

Good Housekeeping

The 1993 Tristar Pictures film *Rudy* is an inspirational true-life story about a young man who refuses to allow circumstances to dictate the course of his life. With a deficit in physical size, athletic talent, and academic ability, force of will alone earns him not only admission to the University of Notre Dame but also a defensive position on the practice team squad; these are the players who run the opposition's plays in practice sessions. As the story reaches its conclusion, Rudy is allowed to dress for the final game against Georgia Tech, something very unusual for a mere practice team player.

In the locker room before taking the field, he and his teammates listen as Coach Dan Devine (played by actor Chelcie Ross) gives his team a pep talk. Coach Devine says: "No one, I mean *no one*, comes into our house and pushes us around!"[15] And while movie makers are known for taking liberties with reality, and the movie *Rudy* contains several of these, Dan Devine is recognized to have made this statement.[16] Devine's statement is powerfully motivating for his players as they anticipate taking the field, and it *should* be powerfully motivating for you . . . whether or not you have ever played football!

In the film, "our house" means Notre Dame Stadium, the *home* of the Irish. As such, this place is considered to be a place wherein Notre Dame establishes the context, sets the pace, executes successful plays, and wins games! For a visiting team to come in and change that dynamic by taking away the authority of the home team is what is meant by being *pushed around* in *our house*.

This paradigm is also a caricature for students in a learning environment, in the classroom, private study, and other places. Here, the *house* is the student's head, the sum total of everything contained in his mindset concerning the learning task at hand. It is what he thinks of himself related to the task: confident, ready for the work, focused, motivated. And just as a football player guards against opposing players coming in to take away these home-field strengths, to defeat him on the field, his *house*, a student must take this same attitude toward anything that might come into his head (his *house*) to defeat him by taking away his focus, concentration, and learning.

For the student it becomes more complex than merely physically beating the player opposite him on the football field. The *student's* opposition, seeking domination in his house, wears many game faces: lack of confidence, belief that the material is too tough, mental fatigue, lack of motivation, friends who distract, lack of focus, and more. *All* of these are trying to get into his house (his head) and take over. If any of these gets in there and stays there, the student is beaten *in his own house*, in his ability to attend to his academic pursuits.

High-performing, elite athletes are taught the mental side of the game from an early age, and they understand how important this aspect of the game is to their success. They become force of will oriented. They learn to tighten their focus and to take complete responsibility for their play. Each player on a football team has a position to play, and his sole responsibility is to master *his* position play. To the degree that every player does that, the team will be successful as a whole.

Too many students (adults included!) have not mastered the mental side of the *learning* game. Many do not even know that there *is* a mental side to the learning game. Just as an athlete does, a student must master *his* position play in this game. His position is *student*, and he must master it just as a defensive lineman masters his.

In a passing play, the defensive lineman's job is to protect his quarterback from oncoming offensive players looking for the sack. The student, in playing his position, has to be on guard for anything coming into his area that *sacks* him . . . takes him off his learning task. Just like an offensive rush can take the defender out of the play resulting in a quarterback winding up on his back, oncoming distractions and negative influences can take the student right out of his learning mind-set, resulting in his loss of his learning objectives. Students, like quarterbacks, can be *blindsided* by oncoming thoughts, ones that have not been stopped!

Each learning venue presents a *position* that a student must play well in order to win at the learning game. He must bring the same power thinking, focus control, and personal responsibility to his *learning* position that the football player brings to playing his on-field position. In short, no one comes into *his* house and pushes *him* around! He calls the shots and determines the results. Elite athletes play their positions well, their teams score points, and they win games. Fine students play their positions well: they score on tests and examinations and they win university degrees. This is Athlete-Powered Learning.

Notes

1. *Out of Africa*, Universal Studios, 1985.
2. *Hard to Kill*, Warner Bros. Studios, 1990.
3. Centers for Disease Control and Prevention, *MMWR, Morbidity and Mortality Weekly Report* 60, no. 35 (September 9, 2011), http://www.cdc.gov/mmwr/pdf/wk/mm6035.pdf#page=21.
4. Centers for Disease Control and Prevention, "Overweight and Obesity," *CDC 24/7: Saving Lives. Protecting People. Saving Money through Prevention*, http://www.cdc.gov/obesity/data/facts.html.

5. Dr. Charles Stanley, "Discipline Determines Destiny," television broadcast, Sunday, May 19, 2013, In Touch Ministries.

6. ThinkExist.com, John Wayne quotes, http://thinkexist.com/quotes/john_wayne/.

7. FOX News Reporting Special, "Charles Krauthammer, a Life That Matters," October 25, 2013, Fox News Channel.

8. Dr. James Loehr and Peter McLaughlin, *Mentally Tough: The Principles of Winning at Sports Applied to Winning in Business* (New York: M. Evans, 1986), 49.

9. James E. Loehr, *The New Toughness Training for Sports* (New York: Penguin Press, 1995), 6.

10. Joel Osteen, *Become a Better You: 7 Keys to Improving Your Life Every Day* (New York: Free Press, 2007), 216.

11. ThinkExist.com, Norman Schwarzkopf quotes, http://thinkexist.com/search/searchquotation.asp?search=Schwarzkopf.

12. Majid Fotuhi, MD, PhD, *The Memory Cure: How to Protect Your Brain against Memory Loss and Alzheimer's Disease* (New York: McGraw Hill, 2003), 171.

13. Fotuhi, *The Memory Cure*, 107.

14. *For Love of the Game*, "Clear the Mechanism," http://www.youtube.com.

15. *Rudy*, TriStar Pictures, 1993.

16. BrainyQuote.com, Dan Devine quotes, http://www.brainyquote.com/quotes/authors/d/dan_devine.html.

Sports, Academics, and a Piano Player

Psychology for Success

S PORTS PLAY a large role in the lives of many people, and there is much made about sports being a *metaphor for life*: playing by the rules, playing fair, not taking cheap shots, respecting your opponents, preparing for contests, being humble in victory as well as defeat, and more. People often make the case that it might be a better world if people lived their lives the way they played their sports, and perhaps it might. But the best one-to-one application of what sport teaches is often overlooked—children's formal educations . . . their schooling activities!

Why is it that sports-oriented lessons are rarely applied to learning academic subjects in school: history, English vocabulary, mathematics, science? With children and parents alike having such high interests in sports, why aren't the lessons of sports being used to teach the lessons of academics? Perhaps it is because neither parents, teachers, nor children see the relationship between playing sports and learning academic subjects. In truth, both sports and academics are animated and energized by identical psychological principles. Well applied by athletes for their athletic performances, it is time that students began to use them for their academic performances.

A word of caution: As you are reading the latter parts of this chapter that deal with classroom and individual study time, you may find yourself thinking: "This is *too* simple!" It is! However, be reminded that powerfully effective strategies do not need to be complicated. Houses are constructed every day with hammers and nails. Striking a sharply pointed piece of steel with a heavier but bulkier piece of steel is hardly complicated . . . but it is *so* effective!

My, How You've Grown Up!

It is not surprising that the influence of college sports upon American culture is in direct relation to the growth of these programs, in all three divisions of the National Collegiate Athletic Association (NCAA), but particularly in Division I (large schools). These schools have experienced dramatic growth in their interscholastic athletic programs, perhaps best exemplified by their football programs.

Today, most all major universities are able to do things that previously would have been financially impossible. With the rise of television viewership as well as on-site attendance, football games serving as perhaps the best example, the money dedicated to sports programs continues to increase. In 2011, almost seventeen million people (per game) watched Division I football on their televisions.[1] That same year, almost fifty million people attended college football games during the season.[2] This game attendance was for the entire 2011 football season and included all schools fielding football teams in NCAA Divisions I, II, and III.

There is good reason why football, and basketball, are termed the *revenue sports* at Division I schools. The dollars that flow into university department athletic coffers continue to increase, and these dollars partly account for the expansion of facilities, scholarship availability for recruits, and a variety of other budgeted items that expand the reach of university athletic programs.

An example of the growth of college athletics is a program called Student Academic Support Services (SASS). *Academic* support for university athletes achieved formal status in the summer of 1975 with the establishment of the National Association of Athletic Advisors for Athletes (N_4A) at Michigan State University. Other institutions quickly embraced this organization countrywide.

Division I universities are particularly prominent in their embrace of the SASS function. While many house their SASS functions for athletes in existing athletic structures such as a football stadium or athletic training facility, many have erected stand-alone facilities for helping athletes acclimate to university life . . . the social aspects as well as the academic. In these facilities are classrooms, computer laboratories, and a variety of learning venues wherein student-athletes study, are counseled by academic/social support staff, and meet with tutors that help them with their classwork.

Coaches stay in close contact with the academic status of each of their players, making sure that their athletes are staying abreast of their studies and the fulfillment of the university's academic *and* behavior requirements. Coaching staffs exhort their players to achieve an optimal performance on the field of play, but there are simultaneous encouragements afforded them in their academic work.

You Think It Before You Do It

On the sports field, coaches both recognize and make good use of recent developments in the field of sports psychology to both focus and motivate their players. What is sometimes not quite as apparent is that these *identical* tools can benefit athletes in their studies. Athletes know that attitude, focus, and state of mind are highly influential in determining their sports performances. But a disconnection sometimes occurs when it comes to their studies. Too many do not know that the *same* elements can have the *same* effect in their academic success, and all aspects of living where striving for success is the proper mind-set. Mind-set and a *right* psychological attitude precede success in almost any venue of human performance, and academic performance is no different.

Who Says So Anyway?!

Joe Namath: "When you have confidence, you can have a lot of fun. And when you have fun, you can do amazing things."

Arnold Palmer: "What do I mean by concentration? I mean focusing totally on the business at hand and commanding your body to do exactly what you want it to do."

Bart Starr: "Athletic competition clearly defines the unique power of our attitude."

Chris Evert: "Ninety percent of my game is mental. It's my concentration that has gotten me this far."

Magic Johnson: "If somebody says no to you, or if you get cut, Michael Jordan was cut his first year, but he came back and he was the best ever. That is what you have to have. The attitude that I'm going to show everybody, I'm going to work hard and get better and better."[3]

All of these elite athletes know that their beliefs, attitudes, focus, and other aspects *of mental toughness* are critical to their success in sports, be it football, golf, tennis, or basketball. And while there are varying views on what *percentage* of their game is mental, all agree that the mental aspect lives large in their performance outcomes. This same *mental* aspect for the achievement of maximum player performance in sports also lives large in student performance in academics!

Getting Your Head in the Game:
Sports and Academics

In his book *The New Toughness Training for Sports*, sports psychologist Dr. James Loehr lists seven criteria for an athlete's achievement of an Ideal Performance State (IPS):[4]

Challenged
Relaxed and calm
Focus
Excited with positive emotion
Ready for fun and enjoyment

Confidence
Automatic and instinctive

Each of these must be *experienced* by an athlete, the presence of each being a prerequisite for the attainment of the highest possible level of performance, that level that is sometimes referred to as a "white moment" performance. While Dr. Loehr's seven criteria for athletic success are widely accepted in the world of sports, they are also powerful tools for people who are *not* athletes . . . and for those who may have absolutely no interest in sports. Their applicability is nearly limitless in terms of the venues they impact. Ideal Performance Strategies are powerful for *anyone* who seeks top performance, on *any* field of play!

Play That Funky Music . . .

An example of the pervasiveness of IPS utility is displayed in the performance strategies of Emile Pandolfi. An elite concert pianist and recording artist, Emile applies the principles of sports psychology to achieve his Ideal Performance State in his concert performances, in the recording studio, and in his extended practice sessions. His unique application of the sports IPS criteria to his on-stage performance portrays how broad, yet uniquely interpretable, the Ideal Performance State strategy is. Emile describes his application:

CHALLENGE
This, I think, is a rare concern. Any discipline worth acquiring has challenge or we wouldn't be wasting our time on it. Perhaps I am different from many people, but I have always found challenges in any music I play. Certainly, there are vast differences in technical problems that each piece presents. But even the easiest tune to play has musical demands that require some thought and imagination. So, regarding being "challenged," I think that that comes from oneself, not only from the obstacles involved in performing the skill itself. One can always find a challenge enough to keep one's interest.

RELAXED AND CALM

Being relaxed and calm, for me, comes from two things:

1. Having prepared yourself as much as humanly possible for the skills that will be required of you. This is a measurable quantity. You can *know* when you have done all you can in the given time. Then you can say to yourself, "I honestly did my best to prepare," so that when you are on the stage (or on the field) you won't be kicking yourself for not having worked harder. That inner scolding alone can ruin a performance!

2. By having the mental attitude that all those people out there watching you are potential friends who want to meet you and see what you have to show them. This is a party—the performance is the entertainment at the party. All your friends came.

FOCUSED

Wow! That's a big one. Even now, after having played hundreds and hundreds of performances, I am newly realizing that one must be focused at every moment during a performance. It has always struck me as unbelievably odd that during a pro basketball game, one of the finest players in the world will miss a free throw. They've done hundreds of thousands of these, and no one is interfering, yet, they do occasionally miss.

Yes there is "life" and accidents do happen, but I believe that—for whatever reason—the player is not focused enough during the actual throw. He is thinking about what comes next. I have been guilty of that numerous times. I am doing something that I can do in my sleep, only—surprise!—I can*not* do it in my sleep, and before I know it, the misstep has happened. I made the mistake of believing it was too easy and didn't require my attention. So, yeah, being focused *every single moment* is essential.

AUTOMATIC AND INSTINCTIVE

I agree that responses must be automatic, because you can never predict what is going to happen during a performance. Every experience is different, so having an automatic response to all the *predictable* aspects is a great help. You have enough to think about without having to remember the individual motions that make up the basics of what you do. Again, for me, that comes from practice. Not just "enough" practice, but way-over-the-top practice that gives you a psychological edge in the realm of confidence.

READY FOR FUN AND ENJOYMENT

This is one of my favorite ingredients in a performance. When I walk on stage, I prepare myself psychologically in this way: I say to myself, "Wow! I have this wonderful music to share with my new friends, and they are just going to have the best time. They will be entertained; they will hear some great music; and they, through their emotional involvement, will be participating with me in this party." At the moment of real-time performance, nothing is serious. If I mess up, I know that that is a job for tomorrow's practice session. I can't do anything about it now, and I just go on with the show. Never let a past mistake turn your attention inward on yourself. Once you get to self-coaching onstage, you are dead.

CONFIDENT

Well, for a start, the obvious answer is preparedness from practice, but there is oh so much more than that involved! When you look at someone, another person, whether you know him or not, whether he is a complete stranger on TV, any person!

What you are seeing is your impression of *what that person thinks of himself.* You are not seeing his stats, his accomplishments, you are seeing your perception of what *he thinks of those stats and accomplishments.* I believe that self-confidence is a skill that can be practiced like any other skill, and that comes, yes, from experience, but also from knowing that you are giving your audience the best of you that you can give at that moment. It does not mean that you will not make any mistakes, it means that you are giving your best. I believe that the *skill* of self-confidence eventually evolves into the *truth* of self-esteem. Self-confidence is about skill. Self-esteem is about integrity.

Integrity is about trusting yourself to do the "right" thing, which I define as those things you believe in. *Integrity* doesn't take practice, it takes self-inspection, and knowing yourself. I believe that a man whose integrity is intact appears self-confident to others, because he likes himself, he has an easy manner that comes from not being (on a personal level) in competition with others. The game or the performance is outside of that; and, yes it can— and often *must*—be very competitive. The just "being" in the space that you are using is coming from a place of complete trust deep inside, and that is a rock that can't be shaken. That is the quiet, motionless place where big, outside actions come from.

ENERGIZED WITH POSITIVE EMOTION

Yeah, this is an easy one for me. I can't wait to do "show and tell," or more appropriately, "show and share," which is how I walk onto the stage. I want people to have a great time. I walk out in the spirit of play, sharing, "Wait till you hear THIS!" My mantra on stage is, "Don't waste their time." So I have done the most preparation I possibly can so that they will be happy they came along for the ride. I honestly love people, and I have something that I believe is worth giving. I believe that *loving people* is interpreted on stage (and probably in life too) as "charm," or "charisma." Charisma is, after all, a sort of *aggressive charm*, and comes from the same place: loving interaction with people. It is not egocentric. Why do some people enjoy watching one athlete and not another (equally gifted) one? Charisma.

SUMMARY

A person who has a game worth playing (challenges that he can master) is truly prepared, and thus relaxed; is focused because *he loves what he is doing at that very moment*; knows his subject inside out; can't wait to get out there and do it because it is his favorite thing in the world to do!; is confident because he truly trusts himself; and is excited to share what he has to give . . . is a happy person indeed, on and off the field. I know because I am one of the lucky ones, doing it in the spirit of play. We are supposed to be having fun. After all, it's LIFE, for goodness' sake! If it's no fun, you shouldn't be doing it as a career.[5]

Performing, whether on a football field or in a concert hall, are two venues of human experience that require *the maximum* psychological advantage a performer can muster. Lots of people are watching, all want to witness a positive experience, and the performer is *the* focus of attention. The presence of very high stakes, pressure to perform, and a limited time to perform can all contribute to a performer's anxiety and stress, working against the achievement of a positive outcome. Without *some* form of psychological preparation, a performer could hardly expect to render a good performance, let alone an exceptional one.

Learning is no exception, and it may be one of the very best venues for the application of what Emile Pandolfi speaks of with regard to achieving excellence in his piano artistry. The activities may be different, but the mind-sets necessary to achieve Ideal Performance States are the same. Playing to win, in both, is always the goal!

Playing Football, Playing Books: What? When? Where?

The same psychological mind-sets apply to playing a sport to win and winning in the game of learning. The reason some do not see this with clarity is because of the physical differences between the two activities, differences that tend to obscure the similarities. At least three differences exist between playing the game of football and playing the game of learning: content, location, and time frame.

In football, the *content of the activity* for the player is doing just *one* thing: individual position play. The *location* is restricted to three venues: the practice field, player meetings, and the football stadium. The *time frame* is finitely controlled in *all* venues by constraints that are established by an outside agent, the National Collegiate Athletic Association.

In academics, the *content of the activity* is student-learned information, information over a wide range of topics. The *location* for the student is varied. In addition to classrooms in a variety of places on campus, the student's individual study time can take place in different places: a dormitory room, a friend's house, a library building, a vacant classroom, or other sites either on or off campus. In addition, examinations/tests may take place in a classroom, via a computer online, in a field experience, or in a combination of these.

A *student's time frame for participation* is unrestricted except in the cases of examinations. NOTE: Some universities or instructors do not include class attendance as a requirement in their evaluations of student performance.

These subject-place-time differences may seem inconsequential, but they are not. Generating an appropriate IPS mind-set wherein the content, locations, and time frames are restricted is far easier than doing so when there is a wide variety in all three. In limited subject matter, venues, and time frames, distractions can be controlled and the frame of focus constrained.

It is obvious that athletes at the university are also students, and so they, too, are similarly challenged to achieve an IPS in their academic studies. The contrast drawn here is intended to show the relative difficulty of achieving an IPS in the *academic* venue, as contrasted to the place wherein this paradigm originated, the *athletic* venue. Notwithstanding this difference, the contrast shows that a psychological system designed for *athletic* performance has remarkable transfer power into a nonathletic area . . . *academic* performance.

Another skill used in athletic performance is also one that is transferable to academics. It has to do with appearance, but far more than just *outward* appearance.

Putting On Your *Academic* Game Face

A football player *wearing* his *game face* prior to kickoff intends to show teammates and opponents alike that he is there to win! But the look on his face is only an external display of a self-generated *internal* strength. Inside, in the athlete's psyche, all seven principles for IPS attainment are in play. The athlete is challenged, calm, focused, trigger ready to respond, ready to have fun, confident, and excited with highly positive emotion. All of these congeal in what he presents to others around him . . . his *game face.*

What teammates see in an athlete's outward appearance is a strong commitment to performance. But that's just part of what game face is about, how it appears to others. What it accomplishes for the athlete is even more important. It provides an inner strength commonly referred to as being *pumped up.* But not too much so.

> The game face focuses and carries the player into combat. Putting on a game face also implies an element of choice and control. If someone "loses it" in competition, they lost their focus and their face

reflects it first. They lose the tuned balance of emotion, focus and skill development that enables them to perform at their best. . . .

Putting on a game face is fundamental to being an athlete or coach, or for that matter being a professional of any sort. Like the Greek insight into play, when we "play ball" we put on masks that help us perform but also change and reflect whom we are.[6]

This paradigm of keeping control while seeking the highest level of performance is portrayed in an interesting scene in a motion picture, the science-fiction love story *Somewhere in Time*. In the story, actress Elise McKenna (played by Jane Seymour) is allowing her composure onstage to become seriously affected by her feelings for the man with whom she has just fallen in love, playwright Richard Collier (played by Christopher Reeve). During her performance, she glances at him and temporarily loses her composure, allowing herself to go off script.

In a dressing-room scene following her mistake onstage, her manager, William Fawcett Robinson (played by Christopher Plummer), cautions her sternly! "Excess within control, McKenna!" he says to her.[7] Both know that her best performance is reliant upon maximizing a highly charged emotional state while simultaneously maintaining strict control of her emotional state.

Like this theater scenario, putting on a *game face* for achieving an exceptional *athletic* performance is also applicable to the attainment of high *scholastic* performance—excess within control! Just as an athlete does the internal work necessary to generate the controlled state of readiness needed to perform in a sporting event, so, too, must a student do the same for any kind of academic event. A student generating the predisposition to perform well in class is equivalent to an athlete getting pumped up for a performance on the field.

While the same principles apply in sports and academics, the *fields of play* on which academics take place are far more diverse than in sports. Taking the seven IPS *sports* paradigms and applying each to two academic venues, classroom and individual study time, these parallels will become apparent. And they will also become manageable.

The seven principles for achieving an Ideal Performance State are: challenge, relaxed and calm, focus, excited by positive emotion, ready for fun and enjoyment, confident, and automatic and instinctive. Each of these will now be examined for its role in these two academic venues.

Where the Rubber Meets the Road!

CHALLENGE

It is important to recognize a challenge when one presents. But even more important is that you know how to react, implementing strategies that will assure that you meet the challenge forthrightly. That's why athletes practice so long and hard. They prepare for anything that may be thrown at them in a contest, with predesigned strategies to meet and defeat their challenges.

The same IPS preparedness necessary for meeting and defeating sports challenges applies to meeting and defeating academic challenges. It's all about getting a response (game plan) in place . . . *before* the challenges occur.

CHALLENGE—CLASSROOM

A student has but *one* task to accomplish in a classroom lecture, to grasp and hold as much of the information presented as is possible, nothing else. This provides a formidable challenge in that the instructor will present a great deal of information in a short amount of time.

In a conversational setting wherein a student is talking with an instructor, such back and forth about the subject matter would allow for an interaction most helpful in gaining understanding. In the classroom lecture, however, the student is playing on the instructor's field, and by his or her rules.

University professors do not function so much in a *teaching* format as in a *dispensing* one. In a lecture hall filled with well over one hundred students, professors have no ability to check for understanding (a helpful teaching/*learning* tactic) but merely focus on dispensing information. This leaves the student 100 percent responsible for dealing with *getting* the information.

A student entering a lecture experience must not only recognize the nature of the challenge, but must own it! No excuses . . . both beforehand and as the subject material starts coming hot 'n' heavy. The student cannot *ever* allow his or her mind to lapse into a "this is too hard!" thinking mode, permitting self-defeating thoughts to arise. Once this thinking creeps in, the challenge becomes the master. As pianist Emile Pandolfi said about fretting about on-stage mistakes: "Once you get into self-coaching onstage, you are dead." This can happen in the classroom also!

And while these thoughts can occur, perhaps as when challenged to pay attention, the task at hand is to get over it . . . fast! When a student allows the *possibility* that the game (lecture, in this case) is just too much, the game is over just as it is in athletic competition. It is called getting *psyched out*, and the concept looms large in the classroom as well as on a football field. Recognizing and coming to grips with the magnitude of the challenge is a first and critical step in achieving an academic IPS strategy.

CHALLENGE—INDIVIDUAL STUDY TIME

The challenge that individual study presents is substantially different from the lecture venue in that the student is in complete control of all of the factors in play. There is likely neither a specified time frame nor a rapid-fire, instructor-driven data presentation to be accommodated. And while this may appear to be an easier venue, it may not be.

When an outside agent is present in a learning environment, such as a professor at the front of a classroom, the focusing process has some assistance. There is one centering focal point, the professor. When the student is alone, the ability to achieve focus is entirely up to the student, absent any such outside assistance. It is the student who must make sure there *is* a focal point.

Here is what the student *must* do to compensate when there is no outside agent, like a professor, to both establish and center focus. The student must: (1) set subject matter–appropriate time periods for study, and (2) establish an appropriate quantity of material for this time period. Absent either or both, the appropriate degree of challenge is neither established nor addressed and the student *floats* through the activity, demanding little and achieving the same.

RELAXED AND CALM

While stress is everywhere in society today, stress is not the problem! Inability to deal with/manage stress is the problem. This is especially true in *any* learning circumstance. If you don't know how to bring calmness to your mind and body in these situations, you will not be able to perform at your best. Classroom and individual study times require that you take charge of your stress.

RELAXED AND CALM—CLASSROOM

A person's body will react to stressful situations via its own biologic makeup absent any chosen interventions imposed by the person. A student entering a lecture hall wherein difficult content material is to be presented by a professor or sitting down to take an important written examination can self-generate stress levels that can go through the roof!

The student feels a tightening of the muscles accompanied by an increased breathing rate, a hotness of the face, and perhaps even an increase in bodily perspiration. A general foreboding sense of doom may be the case for some. If you have felt any or all of these, perhaps some not even listed here, don't be concerned . . . you are among the *normal*:

> The sympathetic nervous system reacts to stress by secreting hormones that mobilize the body's muscles and organs to face a threat. Sometimes called the "fight-or-flight response," this mobilization includes a variety of biological responses, including shifting blood flow from the limbs to the organs and increasing blood pressure. The stress response does not require an emergency; it can be triggered merely by everyday worries and pressure. In contrast, the relaxation response releases muscle tension, lowers blood pressure, and slows the heart and breath rates.[8]

A state of calm is an important consideration in addressing any task. It is normal that when confronted by a formidable challenge, feelings and demeanor change inordinately. You may become anxious, nervous, and generally ill at ease. Test taking is an event wherein virtually all students experience these phenomena. As important as content mastery is for achieving a good testing result, state of calm can be just as important in facilitating the *access* to mastering content. What is true for children is true for adults as well: "The better a child can stay calmly focused and alert, the better he integrates the diverse information coming in from his different senses, assimilates it, and sequences his thoughts and actions."[9]

In an emotionally charged classroom lecture or testing situation, the Making Up Crap strategy is an effective way of doing this, for an ironic reason. Making Up Crap makes use of the same emotions, the ones that render you nervous and unable to remember content information, to *make you* remember content information. The wacky thinking of MUC channels your emotions for a positive result rather than allowing them to result in a negative one.

Finding your own unique tactics for reducing your stress level in the classroom setting is a must! Football players know that the first few minutes of the game will be those wherein they will likely not be playing their best game. They have yet to gain control of their tension and nervousness at that time. Once the game is underway and a few hits have been delivered or received, they settle down and their performances come under their control. In this situation players have the benefit of a physical action (the hits) bringing about a centering of focus and calm.

For the student absent these physical stimuli, he or she would do well to engage in some up-front action to become calm and centered, before being *hit* by the academic challenge. Taking charge of a stressful environment, before stress results from it for you, is the means of being relaxed and calm.

RELAXED AND CALM—INDIVIDUAL STUDY TIME

Unlike the classroom situation, one's individual study time is not very likely to produce a similar level of anxiety and stress as is experienced in a classroom test-taking situation. In individual study time, often the challenge is to *increase* your energy level and degree of excitement. The prospect of siting down for a few hours to read and/or study content material is rarely intrinsically exciting for most students. Especially is this true at the times when it often occurs, after an evening meal! So for individual study, you may find that you are a bit *too* relaxed and calm!

Generating some positive self-talk about the task at hand may be what is appropriate: suggesting to yourself the importance of this particular study time, the value it will bring, the preparedness it will provide for your grade outcome, that it is just "x" number of minutes out of your evening, and more.

Perhaps a brisk walk or some physical activity would help you get *up* for studying, elevating endorphin levels so that the necessary energy is present to perform. Just as it is with calming yourself down, getting yourself up and energized can take different forms for different people. Find one that works for you, and your performance will improve, both in the classroom and in your personal study time. Whatever you do, do not assume that your energy level is unimportant *just because you're not in a classroom*. Take steps, whatever they may be for you, to achieve your own best energized mind-set.

The principle of achieving a calm demeanor is effective for *all* ages. In Synergistic Thinking, the *senses* are critically important for learning and remembering, for taking in information, organizing it, filing it, and bringing it up once again. A state of centeredness and calmness facilitates these. Take the time needed to get yourself there, first, and you will be surprised how much more you are able to learn and retain.

FOCUS: SOME THINGS TO CONSIDER

This is an issue that deserves very special attention. While perhaps not a large one for athletes, it may be the *most* difficult for students in their studies. One reason that it is not as difficult for athletes is that, in practice as well as game time, coaches are present to exhort, encourage, and direct players' behaviors. In the academic arena, students have to make it on their own. Another reason is that most people have never been taught that focusing is a skill that can and should be learned.

They don't know how to do it because they have not been shown how to do it!

Childhood is the optimal time to teach the skill of focusing. Unfortunately, most children just are just told, "Pay attention!" But they're not told how to do it. Children, and especially very young children, have quite good focusing ability. The problem is that their focus ability is centered on just one thing . . . themselves!

Very young children are uniformly unaware of what life will demand of them as they grow older. They are perhaps the most egocentric, self-absorbed people on earth! They see everything as though they are the center of the universe . . . all activity and life orbiting around *them*. The idea of "other" is not inborn, but learned. And the lessons are sometimes painful, as children experience a wide variety of social interactions with others that life brings their way.

Being very young allows a child to get by with a limited focus. There is a pervasive lack of awareness of things outside of the *self*. Peer pressure, what others think, personal responsibility, differences in the sexes, and self-image are but a few issues yet to occur to the very young. Adding to these awareness deficits is the fact that virtually *everything* is intrinsically interesting to children, because nearly everything is *brand new*. For the very young, there's really no need to pay attention, focus, on any one thing. It's *all* fun!

As a child becomes an older and hopefully more mature public school student, and certainly by the time college experience occurs, the full range of potential distractions are fully in play. They are just waiting to steal attention from study and toward a range of new and interesting matters: music, playing games, watching favorite TV shows, interaction with friends, relationships, and sex just to name a few. These distracting influences have to be addressed if productive study is desired. A Bible passage is apropos: "When I was a child, I spake as a child, I understood as a child, I thought as a child: but when I became a man, *I put away childish things*"[10] (emphasis added).

As in this verse from scripture, the idea of "putting away" something has relevance to increasing focus. In a way, a university student (or any student) lives in two worlds. One world, the world of everyday living, contains all of the things that happen during the day: conversations, friends and relationships, places, activities of all kinds. All of these things compete for available time, overlap and intertwine with each other, and cause a constant shifting of focus from one thing to another.

And while focus is always shifting in the everyday world, there is only one *object* of focus in the learning world . . . taking in and remembering information, learning! In the world of learning, like stated in Ecclesiastes, you must "put away" all of the *objects* (those that will surely distract you) of the everyday world, and focus on just one thing in your learning world. Interestingly, this *putting away* of childish things referenced by Solomon in Ecclesiastes is exactly the *adult* attribute necessary to being a good student.

FOCUS—CLASSROOM

A student entering a classroom to hear a professor speak on a less-than-interesting topic *requires* the presence of a *focus-control* game face if any learning is to take place. Distractions abound! The time is limited! The professor is not about to offer a *do-over*.

Professors make the assumption, erroneous as it may be, that students come to class with the prerequisite maturity and interest to pay attention to the subject-matter content that they present. As previously stated, professors are typically not *teachers* in their instructional style, but are just *presenters* of information. It's up to the student to figure out a way to *learn* what's merely being presented.

Some people use the roll-top desk tactic to eliminate or reduce distracting issues. A person may have had a seriously disruptive disagreement with a close friend, maybe even in a love relationship. This can wreak havoc if it remains in the conscious mind. Visualizing a large roll-top desk with its many small pocket drawers along the top provides a good way to deposit distractions temporarily, during the classroom lecture at least. Just envision taking the issue at hand that is distracting, opening one of the little drawers and popping it in, then closing the drawer securely. The visualization trick is remarkably powerful, and its power increases as the tactic is practiced over time. Once out of the lecture hall, the drawers can be reopened and the information therein considered once again.

Another obvious yet powerful focusing tactic is to *stare* at the professor who is giving the lecture. Keep your gaze centered on that professor's face! The act of tightly restricting your view focuses your attention in one place, the professor's face and the words that come out of it! While getting more of the content from the presentation, an additional benefit is that it also lets the other person know that you are *really* interested in what is being said. There can also be an additional relational benefit to this practice.

In a small classroom setting where the student is close to the professor, this focusing tactic can be helpful to the student. It conveys to the professor the kind of interest that professors like to see in their students. This kind of perceived interest can be helpful should the student need to speak with the professor at some later time, perhaps to ask for a point of subject-matter clarification.

There are many more strategies to be applied in getting a right focus, before the professor begins to talk as well as during the lecture. The important thing is that these tactics have to be *volitionally* engaged. They most certainly will not occur if you don't make a choice to make them happen.

While the presence of a person (a professor) talking at the front of the room may serve as a stimulus to you to pay attention, it is a weak prompt at best. Unlike a one-on-one conversation with another, in a lecture hall you are among many and there is abundant room to *hide*. Individual response to what is being said is not required, and you can sit back knowing that no response on your part will be required. Absent this, you still have to make focus happen!

Finally, it would be counterproductive to leave a discussion on paying attention/focusing without addressing an activity that is a problem for many students: *note taking*. Taking notes in class as the professor lectures is common today. But taking notes is a highly ineffective way to grab onto the information being presented.

Note taking is inefficient for one reason: You cannot pay attention to two things at the same time. If you are paying attention to the professor's words, you cannot simultaneously be paying attention to writing those words on a page. It's that simple! Your brain cannot perform two *cerebral* functions at the same time. "Cerebral" is the key!

Some people dispute this and suggest that people who are so-called multitaskers are an exception. But is this true?

> When most people refer to multitasking they mean simultaneously performing two or more things that require mental effort and attention. Examples would include saying we're spending time with the family while we're researching stocks online, attempting to listen to a CD and answering e-mail at the same time, or pretending to listen to an employee while we are crunching the numbers. What most people refer to as multitasking, I refer to as "switchtasking." Why? Because the truth is we really cannot do two things at the same time—we are only one person with only one brain. Neurologically speaking, it has proven to be impossible. What we are really doing is switching back and forth between two tasks rapidly, typing here, paying attention there, checking our "crackberry" here, answering voicemail there, back and forth, back and forth, at a high rate. Keep this up over a long period of time, and you have deeply engrained habits that cause stress and anxiety and dropped responsibilities and a myriad of *productivity* problems. It's little wonder so many people complain of increasingly short attention spans.[11]

This is the view of author/writer/speaker David Crenshaw (author of *The Myth of Multitasking*), who consults with business people whose purpose it is to increase their productivity and efficiency.

If you try a simple experiment, you will see that he is correct. The next time you are having a conversation with another person, try talking to the other person at the same time that he or she is talking to you. What you will discover is that you cannot say your piece while, at the same time, listening to his or her piece. You can't talk and listen at the same time. Your brain simply cannot process both *cerebral* functions simultaneously. It is, as Mr. Crenshaw says, neurologically impossible!

With this is mind, that the mind cannot process two *cerebral* things simultaneously, why would you believe that you can listen and write at the same time; listen to the professor's lecture while, at the same time, writing down what he or she is saying? You can switch from one to the other (switchtask), but you cannot do both at the same time. The reality is that while you are writing what the professor just said (taking notes), you are not hearing (mentally processing) what he or she is *currently* saying while you are writing. You are missing it because your brain is cerebrally engaged in what you are writing. So what's the solution?

As professors are not apt to stop talking or even slow down, you must somehow be able to either (1) listen all of the time, or (2) take notes all of the time. But this cannot work, because in order to write down notes, you'd have to listen, so that you would have something to write. A real conundrum . . . unless you have a pocket voice recorder!

Take a voice recorder to class. By turning on your recorder at the start of the lecture you can devote 100 percent attention to what the professor is saying, knowing that *everything* is being recorded for your future reference if you need it. In this way, no points will be missed while you are trying to take notes. Later in the evening during your individual study time, you can skip through the recording and listen *only* to those points that might be unclear from what you heard during the lecture.

A recorder solution is one that need not be used in *all* your classes, as some may not be so content rich as to require this. However, in the very challenging, content-packed classes where the information is coming fast and furious, a recorder not only allows for another shot at the information later in the evening but also allows you to be 100 percent undistracted in listening to the lecture. With no note-taking distraction, you will get a great deal more information as you are listening with much greater focus and intensity.

Some people will say that it is highly unconventional to sit and *just* listen in class. This alone may be initially anxiety producing. After all, students have been taking notes forever! To suggest that you should stop doing this is educational heresy! However, the reality is that *the proof of the pudding is in the eating.* If you can muster the courage to try this strategy in a difficult class, the results will be immediately apparent. Heresy aside, this works!

If you are thinking that this method makes you listen to each lecture twice, this is not true. With recording devices' features available today, you can skip past what you already understand from a lecture and go directly to those parts that were not so clearly understood, listening to them only.

NOTE: It might be worth stating the obvious here: this methodology will not work if the recorder is never turned on again once the class is over!

FOCUS—INDIVIDUAL STUDY TIME

As difficult as it can be to generate a proper focus in a lecture hall, it can often be even more taxing to do so in private study time, because the number of distracting influences are often more numerous. First, the settings for individual study can be many and varied: one's dorm room, the library, a coffee house, a communal study area, a dining hall. Each venue presents its own set of distracting influences.

Selecting the *right* venue for effective individual study is a matter of knowing yourself and what you need to have in order to be productive. If the presence of other people, regardless of how many, is a distraction for you, don't go there! Stick with a setting wherein solitude is a given. If ambient noise is a distraction, seek out a location wherein it is reduced or absent. One college student told how he was able to escape the madness of dorm life in the evening, finding the right atmosphere for his study time. It was about deception!

After dinner when rowdiness on his dormitory floor was at a peak, this clever young man packed his books and headed for a building on campus a short distance away. In this building were several small study rooms, each with a table and two chairs on opposing sides; two students could use the room at the same time. Getting there early enough, right after the evening meal, assured him of finding one of these rooms yet unoccupied.

He'd enter the room, close the door behind him, and sit down in one of the chairs. But before beginning his evening of study, he'd place his coat on the chair back opposite where he was sitting. He's also place an open book, paper, or notebook on the desk surface fronting that chair. This gave the appearance that *two* people occupied the room. The space was his, alone and uninterrupted for the evening! Sneaky, yes . . . but highly effective in providing a distraction-free study place!

The number and nature of distractions that impact each person seeking productive study time need to be taken into consideration . . . *before* study is engaged. As in real estate sales, "location, location, location" should be the guiding principle in selecting an appropriate place for study. Once the right *place* is found, ridding yourself of internal mental distractions can be addressed by the methods referenced earlier.

EXCITED BY POSITIVE EMOTION

It's not difficult to see the excitement and emotion of football players as they converge on the sideline, pre-kickoff, for the big game. Slapping each other on the butt, high-fiving, and an abundance of trash talk are not-so-subtle indicators of their state of readiness to "kick ass and take names," as the sport-competition metaphor goes. And as so many sports psychologists state, the *mental* part of the game is often the best single predictor of success.

> Your performance is profoundly influenced by your thinking—by the things you imagine and say to yourself. Thoughts are powerful—thoughts make things happen. Every performance starts in your mind. The best performances occur when you take control of your thinking. All control begins by taking control of the thoughts you think.
>
> Champions give themselves a mental edge by standing guard at the door of their mind—by taking control of their thinking and by *deliberately choosing* to focus on the positive.[12] (emphasis added)

Absent the rear end and hand slapping, this form of positive emotion can have a similarly positive impact in achieving readiness to perform in the classroom. The phenomenon of being excited by positive emotion has benefits reaching far beyond the playing field of sport to virtually every playing field in life. The message is both simple and powerful! You *can* change your state of mind by some very simple volitional acts: "So you smile when you're happy, grimace when you're angry, and frown when you're upset. But it turns out that the transmission of nerve signals runs both ways. That is, you can feel better as a result of smiling, become angry merely by grimacing, and get annoyed just by frowning."[13]

Henry Ford recognized the same power of attitude in the business of building cars, suggesting a forthright formula for achievement: "If you think you can do a thing or you can't do a thing, you're right."[14] The late Dr. Norman Vincent Peale was one of the very first to tap into this wellspring of power in 1952 with the publication of his landmark book *The Power of Positive Thinking.*[15]

During the 2012 football season number-four-ranked Notre Dame traveled to Oklahoma to play the Oklahoma Sooners. While Notre Dame was undefeated at that point in the season, many were predicting that the Sooners would have their way with the Irish. The outcome was a surprise to some as the Irish defeated the highly ranked Oklahoma team 30–13. Manti Te'o, a standout linebacker for the Irish, described how it happened in a postgame interview: "We knew what we could do. Today's no surprise. We knew that if we came to work, we came into today with confidence and everybody doing their job that we would be fine. *I'm glad we came out the right way*"[16] (emphasis added).

Coming out the right way is all about taking on a positive attitude of belief *ahead of time,* not as the ball leaves the toe of the kicker at the start of the game. Line blocking, tackling, and other physical skills have to be mastered by football players. But the *head* part, the psychological part of the game, is perhaps even more important. And while sports psychologists and coaches alike have capitalized on this power for improving athletic performance, teachers and students seem to have been remiss in not getting the message for achievement in the classroom. The connection between getting athletes *up* for a contest and getting students *up* for academic performance is often overlooked.

EXCITED BY POSITIVE EMOTION—CLASSROOM

An attitude energized by positive emotions, one giving a student the message that he will get every word that the professor speaks, that he will leave the room with the information necessary to get a high grade in the class, has to be generated *before* the lecture begins. A student getting *up* for a professor's lecture is just as important as an athlete getting *up* for a game. And just as the athlete works on getting up for a game in the locker room and in the pregame warm-ups, a student can accomplish the same result on the walk to the lecture hall.

When "game time" arrives, readiness to perform has to be in place. Adequate preparation via the right amount of dedicated study time, a good night's sleep before the class day, adequate nourishment, and affirmations spoken on the way to class are all additives that make a difference once arrival at the classroom door is at hand. It's all about convincing yourself that you are ready to perform, because you have done what you needed to do.

However, this one can be tricky! You can't fool yourself into believing that you've done your prep work when you have not. The key to positive self-talk is that you have done the needed work, ahead of time, so that you can believe the positive self-talk about having done the work. It is as when Emile Pandolfi says that he knows he'll give an excellent concert performance because he knows that he's put in the necessary up-front practice time to do so.

EXCITED BY POSITIVE EMOTION—INDIVIDUAL STUDY TIME

After a long day of classes, social interactions, and an evening meal, the idea of sitting down to crack the books can be a less-than-enticing prospect. An hour or so of mindless television, chatting with friends, or just relaxing are probably all more desirable as you envision the evening that lies ahead of you. It is at these times that you need to *gin up* the positive attitude (emotions) needed to do what is not your first-choice option. An *emotional* commitment, a "Just Do It!" mind-set, is all that is needed to get you on your way to a productive evening study session. As it is upon entering a classroom lecture, it is just a matter of deciding to decide what your attitude will be.

READY FOR FUN AND ENJOYMENT

"Are we having fun yet?!" It's a common question you hear when it is all too obvious that you are not! Not so obvious is that fun is usually *always* part of the equation for *any* activity that is said to be enjoyable. Winning is always fun, losing not so much. That's because the components of "fun"—mirthful sport, amusement, and playfulness—are not typically a part of losing.

You are hardwired to feel better when smiling, to perform better and to have more fun. The reverse is also true. Putting on a smile *creates* a positive attitude, which results in more fun and enjoyment. "Form

Follows Function" is a paradigm originally stated as it relates to the physics of modern architecture and industrial design.[17] However, this principle, while originally applied to inanimate objects, has powerful implications for human behavior as well.

In the design of a racing car, what you want to get is speed . . . the *function*. The means of attaining speed would include a powerful motor to generate the speed and a sleek design to reduce wind resistance, the *form*. The appearance of the car, or its *form*, is determined by how you want it to *function* . . . to go fast! Similarly, for an athlete to *function* as an outstanding performer, the psychology of the seven principles of attaining an Ideal Performance State must *form* in the athlete's mind.

For a player to play his best game, to attain his Ideal Performance State, he must incorporate, in his performance, the seven IPS criteria. His psychological mastery of these IPS criteria is not a part of his play but is how he accomplishes his play. Similarly, a student prepares for his *best game* in a classroom lecture or in private study time in the same way. The form, the mind-set, that a performance will take on derives from what the student wants to achieve, a high *function* of academic success.

If humor has a positive effect on your ability to perform better either in sports or academic venues, then making a decision that you are going to be of good humor (happy) increases the likelihood for a productive performance. The methodologies for establishing a positive mind-set are identical for both the classroom and individual study. *Getting happy*, as a personal decision, knows no constraints of time, place, or situation. A "Just Do It!" attitude is again all that is needed, in the classroom as well as individual study time.

CONFIDENCE!

The two venues, classroom and individual study time, are different when it comes to confidence. In the first, you either have it or don't have it; you can't *make* it happen! In the other, you make it happen.

CONFIDENCE—CLASSROOM

If you are trying to tell yourself that you are *confident* that you will do well on a biology exam, you can't fool yourself into believing this if you did not prepare by studying for the exam. You know too much! Therefore, you cannot *be* confident. You can fake it to others, putting on a face of confidence, but not to yourself! You *know* what's really *behind* the face, the face that others only see. You cannot, like other IPS factors, make it happen by sheer force of will.

You can cause yourself to gain a state of awareness of a challenge, you can bring about calmness, decide to have a tight focus, become excited by positive emotion, and decide to have fun. All are choice-related operations that you can *cause* to happen at any point by adopting specific strategies. But unlike any of these, achieving confidence cannot be brought about by mere *choice*. Test taking is a good example. If you are to adopt an attitude of confidence, confidence in your ability to perform well, there are some things that you have to have done ahead of time. Studying! In short, you have to have "done the work" in order to be able to engage the IPS confidence strategy.

CONFIDENCE—INDIVIDUAL STUDY TIME

Unlike the test-taking situation wherein a high confidence level depends upon the up-front work, this *is* the up-front work. You *can* decide to be confident about approaching it. For example, as you prepare for a study session, one that you know is critical for learning material you need to know, you can decide that you *will* be successful in studying. You can *decide* to "put on your thinking cap" in a forthright manner. You can *gin up* confidence for the task at hand by performing some mental self-talk, talk that promotes your will to achieve what must be done. Unlike the test-taking venue, you have the luxury of time to achieve the desired results, results that will build more confidence that will serve as a stimulus for even more results.

AUTOMATIC AND INSTINCTIVE RESPONSE

"He has good instincts! He always seems to know where the ball is going and be there to make the hit." "Seems like he's on autopilot!" You've heard this kind of description of an outstanding linebacker, descriptions of near-automatic responses that invariably result in excellent position play. With this kind of performance on the field, it is almost a given that this player prepared himself for the game by acknowledging the challenge before him: becoming relaxed and calm at game time, achieving a high degree of focus for the game, becoming excited by his positive emotions at game time, and being ready to have a very good time doing what he knew he was prepared to do . . . being confident!

You recognize that this player has locked in place *six* of the seven psychological attributes that he needs to play his best game, to achieve his Ideal Performance State. The one attribute remaining, being able to act automatically/instinctively, comes to him *as a result* of having these six already ensconced within his psyche. With all seven in place, he is said to be *psyched up* for the game, and he is!

Like confidence, automatic-instinctive performance cannot be ginned up. It comes as a result of having done the advance work. If the six IPS strategies are operating in a performer, automatic-instinctive responses are possible, in fact, likely.

AUTOMATIC AND INSTINCTIVE RESPONSE—CLASSROOM

In this setting, automatic responses are evident if you have put in the prerequisite study time necessary to have a grasp of the material on which the professor is to lecture. Your assessing the challenge, assuming a relaxed and calm composure, becoming tightly focused, gaining a degree of emotional excitement, and being ready to enjoy the lecture all fall into place *automatically*. As for a football player at game time, knowing that he'll play at a high level because he's done his pregame practice work, you are ready to get the most out of a professor's lecture when you have completed the same process.

AUTOMATIC AND INSTINCTIVE RESPONSE— INDIVIDUAL STUDY TIME

As you are finishing the evening meal in the dorm dining hall, thoughts begin to turn to what comes next . . . *having* to begin that evening study period. Ideally, you begin to mentally process through the seven psychological steps right there in the dining hall while finishing your meal. If you do this effectively, your state of readiness to assure a successful evening study session will be likely, more so than if you just finished eating and then sat down to study . . . no preparation having taken place. If you've mentally put in place all six IPS criteria, your study session will become an automatic-instinctive one to be enjoyed, not an arduous one to be dreaded.

If it seems that achieving *all* of these seven attributes just takes too much time, keep in mind that your continuing to practice them will shorten the time it takes to achieve proficiency in the process. In far less time than you would think, the process becomes a firmed-up part of your game plan, your study habit *pregame* routine. It becomes automatic! Getting this process to be automatic through repetitive practice over time should be your goal.

The "Louisville Lip" Trash Talked, but to Whom?

Muhammad Ali, dubbed the "Louisville Lip," continued to change the worldwide face of the heavyweight boxing division from when he first arrived on the scene in 1964 until his final retirement in 1981. He brought boxing and the heavyweight championship in particular to a level of societal awareness that has been unrivaled since his departure. Everyone, fight fan or not, knew of Ali. Today, most people have no idea if there even *is* a heavyweight champion, let alone who it might be. Ali made the sport what it was . . . the sport didn't make him who he was!

Known for his incredible hand speed and footwork, Ali was even more notorious for his bombastic and endless self-praise, and his often humorous *trash talking* about his opponents. Recall that Ali once said that Joe Frazier was "too ugly" to be the champion! These comments infuriated some and made some laugh, but most never fully understood what motivated Ali to say these things. Ali, now retired and incapacitated by Parkinson's disease and perhaps too many head shots, isn't providing any answers. However, knowing about sports psychology, one answer is both possible and plausible.

Muhammad Ali had a God-given talent that few have had, in boxing or any other sport. But talent was just half of what made Ali the best pugilist of his era. He capitalized on his gift of talent by spending thousands of hours perfecting the *skill sets* needed for such elite performance: footwork quickness, hand speed, punching power, ability to take a punch, endurance, and many more. However, as good as Ali was, there were many others who were well qualified to get into the ring with him, many of whom had the prerequisite abilities needed to defeat him on any given night. Ali was no fool; he knew this very well.

Although no scholar of psychology, Ali had an intuitive understanding of people, both of himself and his opponents. He knew that his opponents were not likely intimidated by the trash talk he threw at them, demeaning their person and skills. He knew what all elite athletes know: that they compete fundamentally *with themselves* for their very best performance, not really against another person. It is therefore reasonable to suspect that all of Ali's verbal assaults against his opponents were really intended for *himself.*

Through his ongoing emotionally charged tirades, he elevated his own levels of adrenalin and readiness to perform, knowing all the while that no meaningful effect would be felt by his opponents. While the term *Ideal Performance State* had yet to be coined, Ali already knew that *he* needed to achieve a level of emotional/psychological readiness to win . . . whatever it might be later termed.

Through Ali's emotionally charged prattle, he brought his personal levels of emotional excitement, confidence, and even his levels of enjoyment to unparalleled levels. And through it all, it was quite apparent that Ali was having fun with all of it! By fight time, all that energy and bombast was pent up inside him just awaiting a powerful release, a release that many opponents experienced as they felt their head and feet change places, rapidly!

Of course, this ascription of intent is only mere conjecture and is unsubstantiated by any available information. As mentioned, Ali himself has never provided any explanation for his behavior. But if Ali knew, as he must have understood through experience, that his prattle was not effective in giving him any *edge* against his opponents, one can only find a few other alternatives to explain it. And many alternative explanations have been bantered about.

Certainly he could have been performing in this manner to generate more publicity for his fights, resulting in larger payoffs. But he didn't have to go so far to get that. He didn't have to *so* mercilessly berate and diminish his opponents while simultaneously exalting himself. Both placed a greater amount of pressure to perform on Ali, a level of pressure that most people would find problematic . . . not helpful. But Ali was not "most people." He seemed to thrive on self-exultation and the added energy-force it provided him.

Perhaps the solution to this puzzle is that all of the "Louisville Lip's" mouthing off was done by him for his own benefit, perhaps his own unique formula for getting up for an upcoming fight. Even if not an accurate assessment of Ali's intent, this possibility comports with what elite athletes today know about the mental side of their sports. Excellence in performance is a combination of the body (physical preparedness) and the head (psychological preparedness). It cannot be attained in the absence of either. The game of academic excellence is played by the same set of rules! Your body has to be prepared, but like in sports, you must have your head in the game!

FOOTNOTE: As is commonly acknowledged, Muhammad Ali made himself known not only as a great pugilist but, as stated, a prolific talker. He never seemed to be at a loss for words, and it was common for him to get the last one! There was one incident, however, wherein Ali met his match in the arena of words. A story is told of a time when Ali, at the height of his reign as heavyweight champion and worldwide recognition, was on a cross-country airplane trip.

After takeoff and having reached cruising altitude, the captain announced that turbulent air was ahead and that all passengers should fasten their seatbelts. Simultaneously, an attractive female flight attendant came down the aisle to see that everyone was buckled up. As she approached Ali, whom she recognized immediately, she saw that he had ignored the captain's request and that his seatbelt was lying unsecured on the sides of his seat. Leaning toward him, she asked politely if he would please buckle up. Ali, with a broad smile, responded: "Superman don't need no seatbelt!" The flight attendant, leaning somewhat closer and returning Ali's warm smile, said, "Superman don't need no airplane *either!*" Still smiling, Ali buckled up.[18]

Notes

1. Frank the Tank's Slant, College Football TV Viewership Statistics, 2011, http://frankthetank.wordpress.com, posted February 2012.

2. 2011 College Football Attendance (for all NCAA Men's Varsity Teams), http://espn.go.com/college-football/story/_/id/8936389/college-attendance-slightly-record-2011-ncaa-says.

3. BrainyQuote.com, Joe Namath, Arnold Palmer, Bart Starr, Chris Evert, Magic Johnson, http://www.brainyquote.com/quotes/type/type_athlete.html.

4. James E. Loehr, *The New Toughness Training for Sports* (New York: Plume, 1995), 7.

5. Emile Pandolfi, Magic Music Productions, P.O. Box 26088, Greenville, SC 29616, http://www.emilepandolfi.com (email to Richard Giordano, September 27, 2012).

6. "Put on a Game Face: Players & Coaches," *Point of the Game*, Monday, September 26, 2011, http://pointofthegame.blogspot.com/2011/09/putting-on-game-face-players-coaches.html.

7. *Somewhere in Time*, Universal Pictures, 1980, based upon the novel *Bid Time Return* by Richard Matheson (New York: Buccaneer Books, 1995).

8. Daniel Goleman, "Relaxation: Surprising Benefits Detected," *New York Times*, May 13, 1986.

9. Canada Education Association, "Self-Regulation: Calm, Alert, and Learning," http://www.cea-ace.ca/education-canada/article/self-regulation-calm-alert-and-learning.

10. The Holy Bible, First Corinthians 13:11, King James Version.

11. David Crenshaw, "The Myth of Multitasking: How Doing It All Gets Nothing Done," http://www.evancarmichael.com/Productivity/3257/The-Myth-of-Multitasking-How-Doing-it-All-Gets-Nothing-Done.html.

12. Jeffrey Hodges, "Champion Thoughts, Champion Feelings," *Sportsmind. Imagine. Believe. Fly*, http://www.sportsmind.com.au/Article-Champion-Thoughts-Champion-Feelings.php.

13. James Loehr and Peter J. McLaughlin, *Mentally Tough: The Principles of Winning at Sports Applied to Winning in Business* (Lanham, MD: M. Evans, 1986), 60.

14. Quotations Page, Henry Ford (attributed), http://www.quotationspage.com/quotes/henry.ford.

15. Dr. Normal Vincent Peale, *The Power of Positive Thinking* (New York: Fireside/Simon & Schuster, 1952).

16. Jeff Latzke, "No. 5 Irish Stay Unbeaten, Top No. 8 Sooners 30–13," *Washington Post*, October 28, 2012, http://www.washingtontimes.com/news/2012/oct/28/no-5-irish-stay-unbeaten-top-no-8-sooners-30-13/?page=all.

17. Florian Fischer, "Origin and Meaning of Form Follows Function," http://www.begleitung-im-wandel.com/pdfs/FFF_engl.pdf.

18. Snopes.com, "Boxer Muhammad Ali's Refusal to Wear a Seatbelt . . . ," http://www.snopes.com/quotes/ali.asp.

Schools Can't/Don't Do
the Job? So What?!
Parents, It's *Your* Job!

U NCLE COSTANZO, the old Italian patriarch, was not known for his politically correct skill sets, in dealing with anyone! This was most evident on those occasions when he took to *tutoring* the neighborhood children in the ways of the world. While a sweet and gentle man, his forceful voice tone was boisterous, downright threatening to those who did not know him. His way of talking would likely make today's child psychologists, well steeped in politically correct counselor-speak, wretch!

Observing a child to be doing something incorrectly in his view, Uncle Costanzo would, not in a mild voice, make the assertion: "No! Don't do it *that* way . . . Do it *this* way!" The classic TELLING style!

The pages that follow should be understood in the same way. For everyone, particularly *parents*, consider what you are about to read as though Uncle Costanzo were telling you: "NO! Don't do it *that* way! Do it *this* way!" This is a *preachy* chapter . . . do it *THIS* way! It's about how you can help your children achieve in their academics with the same power that they achieve in their sports.

The Prizefighter and the News Anchor

The motion picture *Rocky* played in theaters across the country in 1976. And while it generated a large viewing audience in the United States and abroad, no one would have projected that it would have a life spanning the next *thirty* years, culminating with the release of the final episode in 2006, *Rocky Balboa*. Each sequential episode traced the life of a once hapless club fighter to what he thought to be an unlikely outcome . . . becoming the heavyweight champion of the world and the life he lived afterward.

Most endearing throughout the escapades of Rocky's life was his never-lost comical expression of who he was, a common man with some common deficits in understanding. In *Rocky II*, his lack of vocabulary skills was highlighted in a casual conversation with an associate. In the exchange, Rocky is being counseled by a man for whom he used to work as a *knuckle-buster* collection agent. The associate is giving Rocky advice on how he might invest his newfound wealth, resultant of his having just won the heavyweight championship:

(Associate) "How about investing in condominiums? It's safe!"
(Rocky) "Condominiums?!"
(Associate) "Yeah, condominiums."
(Rocky) "I never use 'em."[1]

Rocky's profound innocence and resultant misunderstanding are so pure in nature that hardly any moviegoer could be critical of him. He is simply doing the best he can with what he has. He does not know how to play *games*, nor does he understand it when others play them with him. He is, perhaps to his detriment, sincerely honest! That is sometimes not the case for some people with intellectual gifts far superior to his.

Two issues of national significance were covered in the American news media, each interlinked with the other as they became stories of national interest: the Benghazi attack in Lybia wherein four Americans were killed by terrorists, and the resignation of General David Petraeus for his acts of sexual misconduct. On November 18, 2012, the Sunday news program *Meet the Press* aired an interview dealing with both issues.

David Gregory, host and moderator, was interviewing Senator Dianne Feinstein, D-California, and Congressman Mike Rogers, R-Michigan, about their thoughts relating to both issues.

As Gregory's questioning turned to the Petraeus matter, he posed a question to Congressman Rogers regarding whether or not President Obama knew of the general's infidelity *before* the election. Gregory's posing the question as he does somewhat reveals his view on the matter . . . that the president had *no* knowledge of the Petraeus situation prior to the election:

(Gregory) "You think the President should have been told before the election?"

(Rogers) "I'm not sure the President hasn't, was not told before election day. The attorney general said that the State Department, excuse me, the Department of Justice did not notify the President, but we don't know if the Attorney General . . ."

(Gregory—interrupting) "That's new! That's news. That the President *knew* before election day!"

(Rogers) "I didn't *say* that. I said I don't know!"[2]

First, it reasonable to believe that David Gregory is a smart guy, a *very* smart guy! Top performance at his pay grade requires an acute sense of hearing and highly tuned interpretation skills resulting in an excellent understanding of his guests' statements. Therefore, it is unlikely that his mischaracterization of Congressman Rogers's words was due to his misunderstanding what Rogers said. From the words spoken in this interaction, it is clear that Rogers said that *he did not know* whether or not the president knew, ahead of election.

Given Gregory's skills, it would appear likely that he was not being genuine, but was playing a *game* via his retort to Congressman Rogers.

Games People Play

In 1964, Dr. Eric Berne published his best-selling *Games People Play*, an assessment of both functional and dysfunctional human interactions viewed through the lens of what Dr. Berne called "transactional analysis."[3] While Dr. Berne intended his book to be of use to professionals in the fields of psychology and psychiatry, it quickly became a success in the public domain, selling well over five million copies. It gave people some new understandings of how, with ulterior motives, communications could be choreographed in pursuit of advancing a particular point of view. One of the games Dr. Berne described is "Now I've Got You, You Son of a Bitch!" NOTE: The protagonists in Dr. Berne's game-playing scenario are defined as the *inflictor* (color White) and the *afflicted* (color Black).

Dr. Berne presents the central theme in this game via a poker-playing scenario: "*Thesis*: This can be seen in classic form in poker games. White gets an unbeatable hand, such as four aces. At this point, if he is a NIGYSOB player, he is more interested in the fact that Black is completely at his mercy than he is in good poker or making money."[4] He is more consumed with his advantage over his opponent, his newfound power to laude his supremacy over him, than winning the hand.

Gaining debating-point advantage through game playing (with an ulterior motive *always* in play) has become common fare in American politics, both in political activity and the media reporting of it, on *both* sides of the political aisle. But game playing has spread far beyond politicians and news commentators. The games detailed by Dr. Berne are not played *just* between individuals today. Today this kind of gamesmanship is engaged by large populations, in a seemingly lockstep form of groupthink.

School Games . . . Not *Just* on Athletic Fields

Rocky Balboa's simple, naive genuineness portrays an openness and straightforwardness that is often in short supply today, particularly apparent when parents try to involve themselves with their children's schooling. Mothers and fathers are often held hostage to game playing regarding their children's schooling by the educational establishment: teachers, counselors, and administrators. This is not necessarily by the design or intent of these educators. It can just exist as an endemic presence within educational bureaucracies, absent design or contrivance.

Games are played in the education of young people as various populations within the culture maneuver for acceptance of their respective beliefs. It's the students' fault! It's the teachers' fault! It's the parents, it's the culture . . . and so on. Those parents who make the effort to stay in touch with what's happening in their children's schools are often frustrated by one game in particular, the *Psychiatry Game*. With parents being unwitting participants in this game, the effects can be potentially lethal to their children's educations. And parents need not play!

The History and How We Got Here: It's *Your* Job? NO! It's *My* Job!

In the early history of our country, the value and importance of a *proper* education was afforded a high place in society, and the function of a child's education was never *completely* outsourced, by parents, to anyone! In the early seventeenth century, a small band of Puritans came to these shores from their native England. Oppressed by the Crown under Queen Elizabeth's reign, they came for a variety of reasons, none more important than religious freedom. Also highly important to these first settlers, and the Pilgrims to follow, was the education of their children. In his powerful documentary, *Monumental*, Kirk Cameron explains why they came and what they did:

> You know what I think is interesting is that they had just left England and left this top-down government system, so when they got here, their idea of education wasn't to send your kids off to a government school to educate them. It was the parent's responsibility to do this, particularly because their worldview was different than the government's worldview, which would have been: "You're a nobody! You're a slave! Just lay down on your back and do whatever the king says." Which is, sort of, the attitude we get in most governments today . . . is you just do whatever the government says, whereas they're saying, "It's our responsibility to educate our kids and teach them faith and internal morality and to understand the importance of faith, just and merciful laws."[5]

The Pilgrims knew well the dangers of a state-controlled education system, and they fled it. Once on safe shores, they reclaimed a religious liberty they believed was taken from them by their government, but promised them by their God: "Train up a child in the way he should go. Even when he is old, he will not depart from it."[6]

Today, more than four hundred years later, parents would do well to revisit the beliefs and the daily *behaviors* of their forefathers. So why do so many twenty-first-century Americans not follow the ways of the Pilgrims? Likely to no one's surprise, it may have a great deal to do with fundamental human behavior.

Human Behavior: Complicated and Dynamic

In the previously referenced *Games People Play*, Dr. Berne characterizes a person's behavior, at any point, as manifesting one of three ego states: (1) parent, (2) adult, or (3) child. He defines them thusly: "(1) ego states which resemble those of parental figures, (2) ego states which are autonomously directed toward objective appraisal of reality, and (3) those which represent archaic relics, still-active ego states which were fixed in early childhood."[7]

Remarkable as it may seem, the profession of psychiatry views these three ego states to be the *sole* factors responsible for *all* human behavior. And these three are not fixed in an ongoing sense, but are highly fluid, changing to address unique social demands: "The position is, then, that at any given moment each individual in a social aggregation will exhibit a Parental, Adult or Child ego state, and that the individuals can shift with varying degrees of readiness from one ego state to another."[8]

To respond in the *parent* ego state is to act as a parent is remembered to have acted. In this state, a person displays behavior characterized by the same body language, emotional states, and behaviors of his or her parents. The *adult* state would be characterized by objective and self-directed evaluation of a situation, resulting in a decision made upon the available evidence, with no pre-prejudicial influences involved. The *child* ego state would appear to be like one that a small child might display in a social interaction: submissive, unsure, and compliant.

If these three states are what everyone has to work with in interacting with others, then people's effectiveness depends upon the response states they select in each situation, as well as their ability to *consciously control* these selections.

Modern Attitudes: Why We're Not Like the Pilgrims

Dr. Berne identifies two common "adult" ego-state *games* people engage when trying to gain the upper hand in social interactions: *Psychiatry*[9] and *I'm Only Trying to Help You.*[10] In the Psychiatry Game, one person either states or infers to another that he or she has the credentials (diploma) to be the one *qualified* to offer services and help. They might just as well be holding a sign that says, "See! My paperwork says so!"

You have likely come in contact with a self-described "expert," one who is all too ready to invoke an official title or document to prove it. However, from your past experiences with this person, you know for certain that he or she is *full of beans*! But for those who have not had your experiences with this person, the self-professed "expert" claim can carry weight. A person claims supremacy over another because of some form of an acquired title: "I'm qualified because I *have* this title, and you're not because *you don't*!" This is the Psychiatry Game.

In the *I'm Only Trying to Help You Game*, the person offering help suggests that the recipient of the intended help is to blame if the helping effort fails, if a positive result does not occur. If a service provider is working with an unaware person, the recipient of the service may believe that the failed result is, in fact, his or her fault, not due to a failure by the provider. In short, the provider may succeed in eliciting a *child* ego state in the person who is not helped.

The Pilgrims refused to accept the Psychiatry Game being played on them by the British Crown. They simply moved *out of town*, across the sea, to a place where *they* made up the rules of the game. They took over the game! In twentieth-century America, such strident action is not so much an option for parents, and when it is, it is much more difficult to bring about. Taking this kind of action might look something like enrolling children in private schools, and that can be financially too costly for many.

Parents, those who would like to "change the rules" of how their children are educated, are often confronted by three formidable issues, issues not confronted to such a high degree by the Pilgrims: (1) a firmly implanted educational establishment that, inadvertent or not, are players of the Psychiatry Game; (2) parental feelings of academic inadequacy to take on such an effort; and (3) time constraints on parents, severely impacting their ability to carry out an alternative plan of greater involvement.

Again, stating that professional educators are players of the Psychiatry Game is not suggesting that this is an act of conscious choice on their part. What is being described is a *circumstance*, not an *intent*. While some may be purposeful players, it would be incorrect to believe that most professional educators foist this game onto parents as a strategy. Whatever the reason for the situation, it behooves parents to *take charge* of their children's education. And this is a realistic goal for *all* parents!

What parents can do, as parents, should not be hampered by the three issues cited. For example: (1) the "expertise" of the educational establishment is often overrated (by parents), tending to cause parents to withdraw from playing active roles in their children's schooling; (2) *all* parents are eminently and uniquely qualified to help their children learn, regardless of their self-perceived *subject-matter* deficits; and (3) the time to carry out such a plan is well within the grasp of all parents, in keeping with their busy schedules.

Finally, there is one hidden dynamic in play that often prevents parents from addressing issues in their children's educations. It is defined as "the New Tolerance." A book by this title presents a frightening picture of how previously acceptable ideas of *right* and *wrong* have given way to a new and destructive way of looking at societal behaviors:

> Fernando Savater, the Spanish philosopher, states in his recent book *El Mito Nacionalista*: "Tolerance . . . the doctrine in vogue is that all opinions are equal. Each one has a point, and all should be respected and praised. That is to say, there is no rational way to discern between them." Or, as Thomas A. Hemlock, executive vice president of the national Lambda Chi Alpha fraternity, explains: "The definition of the new . . . tolerance is that every individual's

beliefs, values, lifestyle, and perception of truth claims are equal. . . .
There is no hierarchy of truth. Your beliefs and my beliefs are equal,
and all truth is relative."[11]

There is little doubt that this form of tolerance is on full display in
twenty-first-century society, nor that it provides a significant underpinning for *political correctness*, a curse upon society rivaled by few others
in recent years. And as part of this cultural dynamic, people find themselves operating under some new and rather unusual rules: "Under the
aegis of the new tolerance, our society has created a new civil right: the
right not to be offended, nor even to have to listen to competing truth
claims."[12]

With this new cultural paradigm in place and all too prominent in
our nation's public schools, a parent wishing to take issue with some
practice at his or her child's school might think a second time. Being
viewed as "intolerant" is perhaps the number-one offense that the
so-called PC Police are looking to uncover in you. The PC Police have
morphed the term *intolerance* to mean being bigoted, racist, homopho-
bic, and lots of other very bad characteristics. Dr. Benjamin Carson,
emeritus professor of pediatric neurosurgery at Johns Hopkins, spoke
at the annual National Prayer Breakfast in Washington, D.C., and he
addressed the dangers of political correctness.

> The PC Police are out in force at all times. We've reached a point
> where people are afraid to actually talk about what they want to
> say, because somebody might be offended. We've got to get over
> this sensitivity. What we need to do in this PC world is forget about
> unanimity of speech and unanimity of thought, and we need to
> concentrate on being respectful of those with whom we disagree.
> And that's when we begin to make real progress. And one last thing
> about political correctness, which I think is a horrible thing by the
> way. I'm very, very compassionate and I'm never out to offend any-
> one. But PC is dangerous! Because you see, this country . . . one of
> the founding principles was freedom of thought and freedom of
> expression. And it muffles people. It puts a muzzle on them. And
> at the same time, keeps people from discussing important issues

while the fabric of this society is being changed. And we cannot fall for that trick.

And what we need to do is start talking about things . . . talking about things that were important in the development of our nation.[13]

The direct translation of Dr. Carson's words to parents who wish to take charge of their children's educations is simple: Just do it! Do not fall prey nor be intimidated by the forces of political correctness, forces so destructive to your child's education. In short, parents should not be willful participants in any psychiatry games.

Movie Dialogue to Remember

The movie *Stand and Deliver*[14] was shown in theaters across the country in 1988. The film depicted the struggles of high school teacher Jaime Escalante and his students at Garfield High School in East Los Angeles. Through Jaime's stubborn perseverance, he gained control of a group of young people and taught them one of the toughest subjects in the entire curriculum, calculus. The film chronicles their struggles together and the ultimate triumph of these students, not only in calculus but also in their personal lives. Not only did the students complete the calculus course, they also passed the advanced placement calculus examination.

And while Jaime Escalante was an expert in calculus, the film made clear that this was *not* what made him such a good teacher. It was Jaime, the man beyond the subject matter, that made him a great teacher. He knew the personalities of his students. He understood them as the young people they were. Parents would do well to grasp this, and take on a similar role with their children! Now perhaps more than ever before, parents need to *stand and deliver* for their children. They need to end their *sit and defer* mentality, a mind-set that has relegated them to the sidelines of their children's educations.

Jaime Escalante had to make a great effort to get to know who his students were . . . as young people. He had to make an effort because he did not know them as they entered his classroom for the first time. In contrast, parents know their children far better than any teacher could *ever* know them! This one factor provides parents a power that their children's teachers, even teachers as good as Jaime Escalante, cannot possibly have. If parents will use this power, their children will learn more powerfully than ever before!

Who? What? Why? Where? When? How?

In the past, schools of journalism taught their students six questions to be asked about all news stories they might write, the answers to which gave readers/listeners an understanding of the news event being reported: "Who? What? Why? When? Where? How?" For example, in reporting on the commission of a crime, questions that a newsprint journalist needed to answer for the reader were: *Who* was the victim? *What* was the crime committed? *Why* was the crime committed? *Where* did the crime take place? *When* did it take place? and *How* was it accomplished? These six issues were taught as the underpinnings of sound reporting.

Parents, if they wish their children to be well and appropriately educated, should ask *themselves* these same six questions: *Who* is responsible for my child receiving the best education possible? *What* needs to be done to get my child this kind of education? *Why* is this kind of education important for my child? *Where* should my child receive this education? *When* should my child receive this education? *How* should my child receive this education? The answers to these questions form an appropriate structure for educating children, and one that brings parents into the center of the process, perhaps a place from which they have been absent far too long . . . much to the detriment of their children.

Who?

Parents know *far* more about their children than anyone else! When parents use an MUC learning strategy with their children, they have a warehouse full of thousands of *things* their children already know, things onto which their children can now attach new learning. As previously discussed, learning a new thing is done easily when it is attached to an old thing. Parents know *all* about the things their children already know. Classroom teachers cannot possibly know about these things because they cannot know the children as intimately as the parents do! Therefore, parents are in the very best position, far better than a classroom teacher, to show their children how to use their *old* things . . . to learn *new* things.

As was previously discussed, helping children learn *new* things is about showing them how they are *like* old things. It is about parents helping their children to form associations and make analogies of the new with the old. Parents help their children form understandings of these relationships by stimulating their children's physical, visual, and emotional abilities. They help their children paint new and colorful pictures of new things based on the old things, their past life experiences. They learn/remember the new things through these pictures.

What?

Kind of like the "Who?" question, the "What?" question is about the intimate knowledge parents have of their children, and how this knowledge can be used to help their children learn new things.

A *great* deal of formal education in the K–12 grades is about learning/remembering facts, definitions, relationships, and sequences of events; a lot of things have to be learned/remembered in order to learn additional other things. All of this is fertile ground for an MUC strategy. Once again, parents' knowledge of their children's life experiences is the most valuable asset they have to play a critical role in their children's learning. Associating the old with the new or making an analogy between the two is a powerful way for children to learn, and parents can show them how to do it!

Bringing up an idiosyncrasy of weird old Uncle Fred might be a strong association point for a child learning a new fact, maybe about the strange behavior of a bird. Maybe Uncle Fred has the annoying habit of jabbing at the food on his dinner plate, like a woodpecker taps on a telephone pole. A parent suggests that this bird's behavior is an "Uncle Fred moment." If this association is made (picture is painted) as the child is trying to remember the *name* of the bird, the child can come to associate the bird's name with Uncle Fred! It's an association that no one else could make because no one would know about Uncle Fred, other than the parent and child!

New "what" things are exceptionally ripe for this kind of association and analogy learning. And as parents know about all the old "whats" their children know, they can be great helpers to their children in learning the new "whats."

Why?

The Making Up Crap strategy, as powerful as it is in learning, is rarely *ever* used in schools. MUC requires that teachers would know things about their students' backgrounds, the things the students already know. But with so many students in so many classrooms, this is an impossibility for any teacher. Teachers can use some common life-experience connecting points, but these are not the *personal* connecting points that have the greatest power for an individual student. Also, classroom time being a factor, too many teachers are not really *teaching*.

Far too many public school teachers, especially at upper grade levels, have become mere *presenters of information*, like the previously referenced university professors. A really good teacher not only presents information but also assists in helping the student *lock it in*—learn it! As every teacher knows, learning is a very personal process that takes a personal approach. There's not time for this in schools today, and so teachers "teach to the middle." The problem is that no child lives and learns in a "middle." It's a fictitious place . . . it doesn't exist! Children learn in their own frames of reference, their unique life-experience frames. And teachers, as good as they may be, cannot know these frames.

Parents *know* virtually *all* of their children's life-experience frames because they have raised their children through these experiences. With this knowledge, they do not merely *compensate* for what teachers cannot know. They have the ability to add an entirely new and unique dimension to their children's learning.

Where . . . When?

It may be that some of the very first formal schools were *logs*! A teacher sat on one end and the student on the other. They had a conversation! It was relaxed, nonthreatening, and mostly a comfortable place for both teacher and student. What better parallel location can be found in American homes today than at the supper table? Parents would do well to engage their children at this relaxed time of day about their schooling on *that* day. It may be that an *in-depth* discussion might not be right for this setting, but parents can learn a great deal about what topic should be included in such a discussion . . . later in the evening, in a perhaps more formalized and yet relaxed time.

Parents establishing a formalized time when their children *know* that they are going to talk about the school day is important! The home is the perfect place to personalize education for children. Parents should set up a time for this, and their children should be conditioned to know and accept that this time will be in play every night during the school week.

With both parents often working, single-parent households, and with other factors in play in homes today, a one-size-fits-all system is not workable. The "when" issue is perhaps the most important one because it can always be put off to another time . . . far too easily. If parents want to *stand and deliver* for their children, they must set this time and then stick to it like glue!

How?

As has been stated, parents have what might be called "proprietary" information about their children, information that no schoolteacher could ever *hope* to have. Parents know all of the personality traits, the quirks, the deceptions (self and other related), idiosyncratic tendencies, behavior problem triggers, and other unique traits of their children. Again, who better to know how to approach a child at any given time and for any given subject than a parent?

A parent can know if his or her child is having a hard time in science class, and why. Attitude is all-powerful for learning, and knowing children's mind-sets toward a learning task is powerful! A parent helping a child to a proper *frame of mind* to learn can often be the healing salve to that child, moving the child away from a fearful state of mind about a particular subject. As discussed earlier, achievement of an Ideal Performance State in learning uses the same seven principles that are used in achieving an IPS on the football field. Who knows better the "how" of addressing each of these than do parents? Answer: No one!

THE Student

Parents, *good* parents, strive to manage, form, and monitor appropriately every aspect of their children's development. From the moment of birth until a child becomes ready to assume adulthood, parental influence is THE most important shaper of what children will become. Why has it become socially acceptable to *give away* something so important as a child's formal education to an impersonal schooling institution?

Because of student numbers, time constraints, and other institutional factors in play in schools today, one child has no greater importance than another to a teacher. While not the teacher's intent nor desire, this is reality in the public schools today. But it should not be allowed to remain this way for the parents of these children! For parents, their children are not "just another student" . . . but THE student! This is why the six questions journalists ask themselves about writing a news story should be the same ones parents ask themselves about the education of their children. If parents will ask themselves these questions, they will assure that the very best *stories* will be written about their children's educations.

Notes

1. *Rocky II*, "Condominiums," YouTube, https://www.youtube.com/watch?v=eSG weaROZBQ.
2. *Meet the Press with David Gregory*, Sunday, November 18, 2012, http://www.nbcnews.com/id/49873855/ns/meet_the_press-transcripts/t/november-dianne-feinstein-mike-rogers-lindsey-graham-raul-labrador-tom-friedman-john-podesta-andrea-mitchell-mike-murphy/#.VAjbYWRdXF8.
3. Dr. Eric Berne, *Games People Play* (New York: Ballantine Books, 1964).
4. Berne, *Games People Play*, 85.
5. *Monumental: In Search of America's National Treasure*, Pyro Pictures, 2012, http://www.monumentalmovie.com.
6. Holy Bible, Proverbs 22:6, New American Standard Edition.
7. Berne, *Games People Play*, 232.
8. Berne, *Games People Play*, 24.

9. Berne, *Games People Play*, 154.
10. Berne, *Games People Play*, 143.
11. Josh McDowell and Bob Hostetler, *The New Tolerance* (New York: Tyndale House, 1998), 19.
12. McDowell and Hostetler, *The New Tolerance*, 61.
13. Dr. Benjamin Carson's speech at the National Prayer Breakfast, February 8, 2013, http://video.foxnews.com/v/2152105947001/dr-benjamin-carsons-speech-at-prayer-breakfast/#sp=show-clips.
14. *Stand and Deliver*, Warner Bros., March 11, 1988, chapter 10.

The Black Student

Countering Destructive
Peer Pressure

RON CHRISTIE is volunteering in a HOSTS (Help One Child to Succeed) program in an elementary school in the District of Columbia. On his first day, he is working with a little boy who seems to have some doubts about what's going on. The boy, probably about six years old, says to Ron: "Is it cool to study and sound and act white like you do?"[1] Six years old, and this little boy is *already* dealing with the *acting white* epithet!

While there is some disagreement about the *acting white* assertion regarding its location and severity, most agree that it is a put-down that is real and present among many populations of young black students. It is not racially charged in the common stereotypic terms of counterposing the races, but it occurs *just* among black students—black students ridiculing their black classmates. The phenomenon of *acting white* is found to be most strongly expressed in mixed-race schools, damaging the academic progress of those black students who strive for academic excellence.[2] Perhaps most challenging is that the charge of *acting white* is founded in a pervasive black culture belief system, one that all too often denigrates academic success.

Acting White . . . How Do You Do That?!

Acting white damages young black students by suggesting, forcefully, that their efforts for academic success are somehow racially traitorous! The charge of *acting white* tells them that they have abandoned their black identity in deference to that which is associated with a white identity. The premise is that white people and black people act (*should* act) differently in terms of how they address their academic studies, and that black students are *acting white* if they are acting more like white people act; that is, that they are diligent in their studies, as diligent as white students are perceived to be. A false concept to be sure, but this form of *turf protection* is not uncommon in youth . . . and even for those older and wise enough to know better!

The unique dilemma for black students is not that academic success is problematic, but that it comes at the price of peer criticism for being associated with a group perceived to be out of favor . . . white students. Loss of friendships can result because the successful black student is characterized as having abandoned his or her societal group and joined with another.

Black Culture and Education

As the common cold is caused by the rhinovirus, black students do so poorly in school decade after decade not because of racism, funding, class, parental education, etc., but because of a virus of Anti-intellectualism that infects the black community. This Anti-intellectualism strain is inherited from whites having denied education to blacks for centuries, and has been concentrated by the Separatist trend, which in rejecting the "white" cannot help but cast school and books as suspicious and alien, not to be embraced by the authentically "black" person.

That this attitude is a problem in inner-city communities is not unknown, but it also permeates the whole of black culture, all the way up to the upper class.[3]

The author of this charge, John McWhorter, spent years teaching at elite universities in a variety of fields: linguistics, American studies, black culture, and others. Of his experiences with black students who have taken his classes at the university and also during his earlier K–12 teaching, he says, "It is not fun to write this; I would rather let these crummy episodes fade into history."[4]

Not relishing his conclusions, McWhorter's central theme is that black students, from all classes, dedicate themselves less to their schoolwork than do other students, without respect to life history or other conditions. Shelby Steele, in his 1990 groundbreaking book *The Content of Our Character*, described how a large number of his black students play into this anti-intellectual image:

> A black student I met at UCLA was disturbed a little when I asked him if he ever felt vulnerable—anxious about "black inferiority"—as a black student. But after a long pause, he finally said: "I think I do." The example he gave was of a large lecture class he'd taken with over three hundred students. Fifty or so black students sat in the back of the lecture hall and "acted out every stereotype in the book." They were loud, ate food, came in late—and generally got lower grades than whites in the class. "I knew I would be seen like them, and I didn't like it. I never sat by them." "Seen like what?" I asked, though we both knew the answer. "As lazy, ignorant, and stupid," he said sadly.[5]

From these examples, it would appear that any attempts to improve black students' academic success will be made in a cultural setting not *generally* oriented to academic excellence. If Professors McWhorter and Steele are accurate in reporting what they have witnessed in their university experiences, black culture not only sustains but in some cases purposefully advances stereotypical behavior that is damaging to the academic success of its youngest members. And its youngest members are major contributors to their own plight!

However difficult it may be to find, support for fighting the anti-intellectual stereotypical image of blacks in their own culture must be found *within the black culture*. But that is perhaps where it is the most difficult. The internal inertia for maintaining the status quo is strong!

Cultural Expectations, School Climate, and *Acting White*

The charge of *acting white* is at home largely in schools where the student population is mixed race, but with a substantial white student representation. Dr. Roland Fryer, assistant professor of economics at Harvard University, pinpoints the populations where *acting white* most often occurs: "The evidence indicates that the social disease, whatever its cause, is most prevalent in racially integrated public schools. It's less of a problem in the private sector and in predominantly black schools. . . . In predominantly black schools, I find no evidence at all that getting good grades adversely affects student popularity."[6]

Student popularity and the social networking of students among their peers are the criteria by which *acting white* is measured in schools. The extent to which high-achieving students are made to feel discomfort for their success provides a measure of *acting white*. The reason for such behavior by the majority of members in the group, the student's peer group, is founded in simple human behavior:

> Anthropologists have long observed that social groups seek to preserve their identity, an activity that accelerates when threats to the internal cohesion intensify. Within a group, the more successful individuals can be expected to enhance the power and cohesion of the group as long as their loyalty is not in question. But if the group risks losing its most successful members to outsiders, then the group will seek to prevent the outflow.[7]

John McWhorter, on record for his view that black culture is largely anti-intellectual, describes how black students *self-sabotage* their learning/schooling. He points to a case study in Shaker Heights, an affluent suburb of Cleveland, Ohio. The schools there are rated as excellent and are funded to the tune of approximately $10,000 per year per student. But even in this environment, black students do not do well, regardless of income, level, or class:

> The Shaker Heights case makes it painfully, but incontrovertibly, obvious that the reason that black children underperform in

school is that they belong to a *culture* that discourages them from applying themselves to books and learning—regardless of income, class, and regardless of the social intervention of even the best intentioned people. The centrality of this factor is quite empirically evident: for example, a black student in Shaker Heights reported that she began as a good student, but that her black friends called her "acting white" and "an oreo" for doing so, and that in order to get back in their good graces she let her grades plummet; meanwhile, a white student at the school felt nothing less than pressured by her peers to succeed.[8] (emphasis mine)

If McWhorter is right about black culture being anti-intellectual, that black youth tend to self-sabotage their learning, and that their peer pressure dictates a lockstep with group expectations, the possibility for academic success is slim at best. But there is yet another issue in the black culture, one that adds to the educational difficulties black children face.

Two Minus One = Less Than More

Two parents, *both* mom and dad, have been empirically shown to be the best family setting for educating society's children; two = better than one. But the family in black culture is all too often missing one of the two parts:

A staggering number of African-American children are raised in single parent homes, compared to the rest of America, and the rest of the world. A study conducted by the Organization for Economic Cooperation and Development found that 25.8 percent of American children are raised by a single parent, a number high above the 14.9 percent average seen in the other 26 countries surveyed. Among African-Americans, the rate nearly tripled, with 72 percent of black children relying on a single parent.[9]

Whatever the percentage number, the single-parent home presents a challenge to *parents* being able to provide the educational support needed within the home . . . if only because the number of parents available to provide it is halved. However, be there one parent or two, there is yet one additional factor that can be detrimental to black children. It is that *black* families place an inordinately heavy emphasis on sports with their children.

> Now, more than ever, African American parents have placed a greater emphasis on their children's success in sports. They often believe that their child has the making of the next great athlete, causing African American children to have the highest aspirations for athletic careers. . . . The emphasis on sports has and will continue to cause many African American children to fail. They are often set up by the mindset of their parents, coaches, teachers, and community. They are told at an early age that they will become a great athlete one day.[10]

Black Student-Athletes:
High Status, but with a *Catch*

Sports has become a high-priority focus in American culture, and much attention has been given to its central figures, the athletes. While there is no such restriction at the professional level, *school* participation in sports (at all levels of play) is dependent upon *academic eligibility* . . . passing grades in school classes. And while the sports playing fields may be level for both black and white athletes, the academic playing field for the black athlete is *tilted* . . . and not in the athlete's favor.

There is little to no argument that black students have gained increased access to universities due to their athletic abilities. Being outstanding athletic performers in their high school years earns them athletic scholarships that pay, in many cases, for all of their college tuition and housing expenses. With one year at a four-year institution costing an average of over $22,000,[11] their athletic abilities afford them access to educational opportunities that they might not otherwise have. Especially is this true for many black athletes who come from the mean streets of the inner cities, where families are frequently fractured and unable to provide such financial support.

But getting to a university is just the first step. There are two additional circumstances that can hinder many black student-athletes as they seek success at the university. First, the degree of preparedness that black students bring to the university is often inadequate, not on par with their white counterparts. Second, the families from which they come often place demands upon them that their white teammates do not experience. Former basketball standout at Indiana University, and later in the NBA both as both a player and coach, Isiah Thomas talks about these:

> There are structural forces and institutional structures at play that, when taken together, unintentionally constrain the ability of black male athletes to graduate. The first of these structural forces is that many black student-athletes come to campus with poor academic preparation. This is often due to the poor quality of urban public schooling in our nation, and reflects recruiting practices and priorities that privilege athletics and not academics, thus putting young people in situations where it is extremely challenging for them to excel academically. Many (though not all) of these black male student-athletes come from high-poverty neighborhoods, and thus face additional challenges in their transition to college. These include needing to support family members at home, struggling to meet their own expenses, and not having the same level of support as other students.[12]

Just Dumb Jocks?

"Only 50 percent of black male athletes graduate within six years from colleges in the seven major NCAA Division I sports conferences, compared with 67 percent of athletes overall."[13] In addition to this statistic for student-athletes in general, black student-athletes draw an even more focused critique. Albert Bimper Jr., assistant professor of special education, counseling, and student affairs at Kansas State University, narrows the focus: "There are beliefs and perspectives that student-athletes are 'dumb jocks,' and that burden is greater for black student-athletes."[14] The *dumb jock* label appears to be in place, at least in universities with large sports programs. However, with all of the negatives that attach to university student-athletes, and to black student-athletes in particular, there is another side to this story, this time a more positive one.

Athletic Participation = Corporate Culture Success!

Employers at a University of South Carolina job-recruiting event were asked to rate the value of experiences of more than a dozen types of students, over a range of college activities. Specifically, who did they routinely like to hire for positions in their companies?

> The employers, which were known to hire athletes, gave high marks to many graduates who held leadership positions. But athletes—particularly those who were captains of NCAA teams—scored the highest. Among the reasons: The employers saw athletes as hard-working and goal-oriented with the ability to handle pressure. Among the other findings: Simple membership on a team was seen as more valuable than managing a restaurant, working as a resident assistant, playing in the marching band, or serving as editor in chief of the student paper.[15]

Athletes, *those who graduate*, are more prepared for the world of work by virtue of the training they received in their sports participation during their college years. They come away with salable skills: they find a way to win, they are resilient, they are strong communicators, they're team oriented, and they manage time well.[16] In addition, the attributes of fearlessness, adaptability, and an ability to handle adversity also make student-athlete graduates welcome additions to the business culture.[17] So at least for those who graduate, perhaps athletes are not just *dumb jocks* after all!

Dr. Jim Loehr originated his Ideal Performance State (IPS) strategies for sports-performance excellence, but they also apply to areas outside of sports—to business executives for example. Loehr applies the same IPS principles to *stars* in the business world as he does to *stars* in the sports world. In business as in sports, he targets the skills of endurance, strength, flexibility, self-control, and focus. "Increasing capacity at all levels allows athletes and executives alike to bring their talents and skills to full ignition and to sustain high performance over time—a condition we call the Ideal Performance State (IPS)."[18] If black students can shed the *acting white* charge asserted by their peers, they will be able to achieve full ignition in their academic performances, just as they do in their sports.

Whatever one might think about the academic abilities of student-athletes, the skills and behaviors that they practice for athletic performance also contribute to making them very good role models for students, and for black students in particular. The psychology behind an athlete's performance has a one-to-one application to black students who struggle with their academics, and with their peers who disparage them for *acting white* in their academic struggles. For both those asserting and receiving the *acting white* accusation, a *cultural* paradigm shift away from this destructive charge would help break this insidious cycle of lower academic performance for black students. And sports may provide a way to get there!

Fighting the Charge

If black students confronted with the charge of *acting white* could know that academic success is a *positive* thing to be valued, not a negative cultural stereotype, becoming a good student would be embraced and not denigrated. Black students would see that there are no "groups" when it comes to being a good student! Learning would cease to be tainted, and black students seeking excellence in school would be freed from experiencing the social contempt of their culture. Opening a new door and entering a room free of bad-mouthing good grades in school is the route to dismantling *acting white*. The *key* to that door is sports!

High school, college, and professional athletes are held in high esteem. There is no racial stereotyping, black or white, when a powerful tailback makes a run into the end zone! As elite athletes are widely held in high esteem, associating academics with what they do translates academics into a positive to be valued, not a negative to be ridiculed.

The Ideal Performance State (IPS) psychological strategies used by elite sports figures can offer a powerful identification issue for black students, one that enjoys broad group support. If black students were to adopt an approach to their studies that their respected athlete role models adopt for their sports, an entirely different mind-set would result—a very *positive* association that carries no racial or group identity charge. Through this association, young black students could effectively insulate themselves from charges of *acting white*. Also, peers who might be tempted to hurl the *acting white* epithet would be effectively neutered. Who could criticize a classmate for acting like an elite athlete?

The task is to get black students, *all* black students, to adopt an IPS sports approach to their studies, and begin to see academic striving and success not through a racial-group-identity lens, but through a sports lens! This *new* lens focuses tightly on those people that they respect and honor, elite athletes . . . and particularly elite *black* athletes. This is the end game that can render the *acting white* charge powerless. Were this paradigm shift to be embraced by the broader culture, including parents, teachers, relatives, and other influential adults, the charge of *acting white* would go out of style. It would no longer fit!

Uncle Costanzo's Wisdom

The previous chapter contained a story about the old Italian patriarch Uncle Costanzo and how he helped neighborhood children stay on the straight and narrow in the 1950s. Not a man of political correctness, even though PC was a term yet to be invented, Uncle Costanzo would have been the embodiment of what was politically *incorrect*! His approach was not to share, cajole, or be gently sensitive to children's feelings. He *told* them what to do! No . . . don't do *that*! Do *this*! A politician he was not!

This is *precisely* the message black parents and other significant people in the black culture need to deliver to their children. Do *not* allow yourself to be taken off course, your academic course, by the negative race-based charge of *acting white*! Don't do *that*! Do *this*! Stay engaged with your schoolwork to the very best of your abilities. Adopt and apply the positive IPS principles used by the very best athletes in the world! DO THIS!

Uncle Costanzo's wisdom, simple and direct as it was, TOLD children how to behave to achieve the best outcome, it didn't leave it up to them. Sometimes children need to be *told* about what is best for them, not asked what *they* think is best . . . as if they might even know! This is what black parents must do for their children in order to help them put distance between themselves and the debilitating charge of *acting white*! *Tell* them: Don't do that . . . be influenced by the charge of *acting white*! Do *this*! *Be* like Michael Jordan! Do what he would do.

I Wanna Be Like Mike!

It is not a good thing that black parents place *so* much emphasis on sports with their children. However, it might be possible to turn this negative into a positive. A television commercial a while ago had an "I wanna be like Mike!" theme. Michael Jordan's behavior, both on and off the basketball court, made him a worthy hero for many young people, and more so young black males in particular. They had a natural inclination to want to be "like Mike."

Even though he is no longer playing basketball, Michael Jordan's popularity, especially in the black culture, remains strong. One need only consider the popularity of the Nike basketball shoes bearing his name. Be they Air Jordan Future Flight, Jordan True Flight, or Air Jordan Retro 2 models (costing over $150 a pair), stores offering these for sale sell out quickly, and often with some unwanted side effects. Crowds of frequently majority-black young people gather well ahead of store openings. Their fervor to own these shoes often results in near riotous conditions. Police are often called in to reestablish order.[19]

It is unquestionable that Michael Jordan's prominence in the black culture persists over time, long after his departure from the basketball court. And while some undisciplined young people insult his example by jostling each other for shoes, there remains a better way to gain a benefit from Jordan's accomplishments, both on and off the basketball court. And it will not cost parents the price of a pair of shoes!

Children are highly impressionable. Parents as well as other connected adults should direct their attention to recognize that Michael Jordan is worthy of emulation not *just* because of his basketball exploits. He is successful as a *man*! He is disciplined and purposeful through *learned* abilities, ones that led him to success in basketball as well as life. Above all, Michael Jordan is an educated man and not a high school dropout. After graduating high school, he went on to enroll at the University of North Carolina. And while he left college to join the NBA draft in 1984, he was a student for the three preceding years at the University of North Carolina. A good question for black parents to ask their children is: "As a high school graduate and a student-athlete at UNC, was Michael Jordan just *acting white*?!"

Michael Jordan is a sports hero that *all* children can hold in high esteem. Superstars like Michael Jordan can be particularly important role models for young black students, not just for their sports performances, but for their academic and life performances. But there are many more like Michael Jordan.

A University, a Basketball Player, and a Little Girl: Success Beyond the Boards

During the 2014 basketball season, Lacey Holsworth, an eight-year-old little girl afflicted with cancer, became an important part of Adreian Payne's life. Payne, a basketball player at Michigan State University (MSU), had established himself as a standout player in the preceding two seasons. But nothing he did previously on the basketball court would make him a *fraction* of the star he was more than his involvement in the last year of a little girl's life. Lacey would ultimately lose her battle with cancer in April of 2014, but her final months were joyful because of this young man with a very big heart! Their brief time together is told in Jason King's report "The Adreian Payne Story: How Michigan State Star Became the Ultimate Role Model."[20]

Adreian Payne's time with "Princess Lacey," as she came to be known, came about as a result of circumstances predating his time at MSU. A poor student at Jefferson High School in Dayton, Ohio, his principal knew what future options awaited him: "He was either going to work to be able to take advantage of his gifts, or he was going to be the tallest janitor we had."[21] Through Principal Richard Gates's tutoring and the efforts of others in Adreian's family, Adreian came to understand that he needed to develop his academic skills as much as his basketball skills, and that he could accomplish both in the same way.

Dr. Gates showed Adreian that he could succeed in academics if he applied the same *mind skills* (Ideal Performance State skills) that he used on the basketball court. And it had nothing to do with acting one color or another! Once he saw the connection, Adreian became a different person in his classes! "From that point forward, Payne embraced academics as if it were a sport, showing the same intensity in the classroom as he did on the basketball court."[22]

All children, regardless of color, would do well to know that Michael Jordan, Adreian Payne, and countless other star athletes apply the strategies of achieving an Ideal Performance State in their personal-professional lives, away from their sports. For black children, this lesson can be even more powerful in helping them insulate themselves from the charge of *acting white*. They need to know that people, especially their sports heroes, are more than just *sports* heroes! Parents and other significant adults in their lives need to help them by teaching them these lessons!

Super-Charged Learning is a strategy for parents to use with their children, at home, and it is most effective when reinforced by *two* parents. As mentioned, the single-parent black family presents a less than advantageous opportunity for success in defeating the *acting white* charge. However, success in the fight against such self-sabotage is not diminished if single-parent families engage the help of others, outside of the home.

Teachers, coaches, aunts, uncles, grandparents, religious leaders, community mentors, all of these play a role in taking up the slack for the missing parent and helping young people to "be like Mike," or whomever else they might see as a positive role models. Adreian Payne was just thirteen years old when he lost his mother, but as with his high school principal, many stepped in to help him to become successful.

Eating the Elephant, One Bite at a Time!

In earlier chapters, the role of Making Up Crap was shown to be a powerful strategy in *causing* young people to learn and remember information. *Bite by bite*, learning takes place absent the usual pain and suffering so often associated with the education process. Large quantities of information are learned by simply attaching the unknown to the known . . . by the bizarre strategy of Making Up Crap.

Making Up Crap is the *process* that helps students get the product, things learned. But a process is of little value unless it is engaged (applied), and students have to *self-generate* a will to *apply* the MUC process. Ideal Performance State principles are the means by which this is done, and it is the task and responsibility of parents and other significant people to teach students, particularly young black students, these powerful strategies. If this is done, student by student, the academic achievement of black students as a group will improve . . . bite by bite!

This is the endgame strategy for improving black student's academic success. When young black children incorporate the attitudes and behaviors of their high-profile athletic heroes into their academics, being accused of *acting white* will become irrelevant to their lives, in school and beyond school!

Notes

1. Ron Christie, prologue to *Acting White: The Curious History of a Racial Slur* (New York: Thomas Dunn Books, 2010).
2. Roland G. Fryer, "Acting White," *Education Next* 6, no. 1 (Winter 2006), http://educationnext.org/actingwhite/.
3. John McWhorter, *Losing the Race: Self-Sabotage in Black America* (New York: Harper Perennial, 2000, 2001), 83.
4. McWhorter, *Losing the Race*, 95.
5. Shelby Steele, *The Content of Our Character: A New Vision of Race in America* (New York: Harper Perennial, 1990), 135.
6. Christie, *Acting White*.
7. Christie, *Acting White*.
8. McWhorter, *Losing the Race*, 123.
9. Kevin Webb, "72 Percent of African-American Children Are Raised in Single Parent Homes," *Atlanta Blackstar*, December 23, 2012, 1.
10. André Walker, "Challenging the Over-Emphasis on Sports," *African American News*, January 27, 2014, 1.
11. Statistic Brain, "Average Cost of College Tuition," U.S. Department of Education, National Center for Educational Statistics, November 23, 2013, http://www.statisticbrain.com/average-cost-of-college-tuition/.

12. Isiah Thomas and Na'ilah Suad Nasir, "Black Males, Athletes, and Academic Achievement," *Huffington Post*, May 7, 2013, http://www.huffingtonpost.com/isiah-thomas/black-males-athletes-and-_b_3232989.html.

13. Shaun R. Harper, "Black Men as College Athletes: The Real Win-Loss Record," *Chronicle of Higher Education*, January 20, 2014, http://chronicle.com/article/Black-Men-as-College-Athletes-/144095/.

14. Albert Bimper Jr., "Researcher Looks at Black Student Athletes' Experiences in College Sports, Improving Graduation Rates," Kansas State University, April 25, 2013, http://www.k-state.edu/media/newsreleases/apr13/athletics42413.html.

15. Brad Wolverton, "What's Better for Your Resume, Captain of the Debate Team or Playing College Sports?" *Chronicle of Higher Education*, April 23, 2014, http://chronicle.com/blogs/players/whats-better-for-your-resume-captain-of-the-debate-team-or-playing-college-sports/34777.

16. Stephanie Vozza, "Why Your Next Employee Should Be a Former Student Athlete," FastCompany.com, April 10, 2014, http://www.fastcompany.com/3028829/why-your-next-employee-should-be-a-former-student-athlete.

17. Nolan Harrison, "Three Traits Athletes Possess That Can Lead to Success Off the Field," LinkedIn.com, April 4, 2014, https://www.linkedin.com/pulse/article/20140404163908-23289025-three-traits-athletes-possess-that-can-lead-to-success-off-the-field.

18. Jim Loehr and Tony Schwartz, "The Making of a Corporate Athlete," *Harvard Business Review*, January 2001, http://hbr.org/2001/01/the-making-of-a-corporate-athlete/.

19. Phil Luciano, "Newest Air Jordans Spark Crowd Control at Northwoods Mall," *Journal Star*, February 24, 2014, http://www.pjstar.com/article/20140224/News/140229531.

20. Jason King, "The Adreian Payne Story: How Michigan State Star Became the Ultimate Role Model," *Bleacher Report*, February 5, 2014, http://bleacherreport.com/articles/1947345-the-adreian-payne-story-how-michigan-state-star-became-the-ultimate-role-model.

21. King, "The Adreian Payne Story."

22. King, "The Adreian Payne Story."

So What Was
That All About?

IF YOU'VE been napping, not paying close enough attention or just drifted away from time to time, hopefully this will bring you out with something that you can use, for your children and yourself. *Super-Charged Learning* is about energizing your emotional, visual, and physical strengths (via wacky Making Up Crap thinking) and animating them through an Ideal Performance State mind-set. If you approach your learning tasks with these tools, you will learn larger quantities of information, learn faster, and hold on to what you've learned over longer periods of time. You will be a super-charged learner! Here's how it all shakes out.

A Songster and a Caretaker

The Kingston Trio achieved instantaneous notoriety with the release of their song "Tom Dooley" in 1958. It topped the sales charts with a total sale of more than six million copies. The three members, Bob Shane, Nick Reynolds, and Dave Guard, sang and clowned around on stage, often telling jokes between songs. In their later years they performed together for the last time. During that performance, Reynolds asks Shane to tell the one about the snail. Shane obliges: "This guy hears a scratching on his door. He opens the door, looks down, and there's a snail there. He picks it up and throws it across the street into the woods. Three months later he hears this scratching on his door. He opens the door and the snail looks up and says, 'So what was that all about?!'"[1]

Finishing up, this same question seems apropos. What *was* that all about? What does Making Up Crap have to do with anything or anyone? And how do athletes figure in? In chapter 3 you were introduced to a man, Doug Aiken, who had a substantial impact on how many young people came to view their schooling/learning. As the caretaker at a summer camp, he was always available for a conversation on just about any topic. Staff members working at the camp jumped at opportunities to work alongside him.

While Doug was a good-natured and agreeable man, he was not shy about correcting what he perceived to be immature or inappropriate behavior. On one occasion a cabin counselor with whom he was working was complaining loudly, saying something like "this damned wrench!" Using an open-ended wrench to loosen a rusted nut, the young man was having difficulty. Doug, without looking up from his work and absent any hint of nastiness in his voice, said, "A poor workman blames his tools."

It has been over forty years since Doug suggested to that young man how silly it was for him to blame an inanimate object for *his* deficiency, and Doug has long since left this world for one far better suited to his gentle nature. But his message remains strong. The young man was ascribing responsibility to an inanimate object for *his* inability to loosen a nut because his tool selection was incorrect. As Doug showed him, he should have selected a box wrench to loosen the nut because a box wrench completely captures the nut and allows for no slippage. He had the tool there on the workbench before him, but he failed to comprehend its application. He didn't *know* enough to select it.

Beyond a Caretaker's Workshop

Being a successful student requires that you *know* your tools. It requires that you recognize and use of *all* of your God-given learning tools, not allowing ignorance or misuse to become an excuse for failure. Everyone is born into the world with the unique gifts of emotion, physical sensation, and the ability to visualize. No other animal on earth has these qualities as powerfully refined as you do. And no other animal has the ability, by conscious choice, to bring them to bear on a task.

As has been discussed, receiving information takes place through linguistic pathways . . . words, words, words! But, *remembering/learning* takes a different path. Remembering what the words mean is enabled by our emotions, physical sensations, and our ability to "see" (in our mind's eye) what we are receiving in words. Making Up Crap is about using *all* of the tools in your intellectual toolbox, particularly those that you found to be *so* important to you as a child: emotion, physicality, and visualization.

As children progress through the grades in their formal schooling, the power of language is strongly emphasized. It's all about *words!* As the emphasis on words increases, children incrementally lose hold of their propensity to *feel, manipulate,* and *visualize* their worlds. Bringing these three *tools* back into play once again adds great power to the language-based nature of learning. In today's classrooms the power of words is dominant, and the human traits that make learning/remembering happen are often overlooked in the teaching process. So if the schools do not adequately teach the power of these tools, who is to do it?

A Mountain Man and a Message

Jeremiah Johnson, a film starring Robert Redford, is the story of a man who leaves civilization behind and goes high into the Rocky Mountains to live in isolation . . . as a mountain man. Aside from frequent battles with the Indians who inhabit the mountains, he has no contact with any form of civilization for years.

In a scene late in the film, a troop of cavalry in search of a lost wagon train arrives at Johnson's cabin to ask for his help in locating the lost settlers. Approaching, an officer attempts to initiate a conversation with Johnson. He receives no response. After a few more tries by the bewildered officer, Johnson laughs! Frustrated and confused first by silence and then by seemingly inappropriate laughter, the officer asks if he has said something wrong. Johnson finally responds: "Ahh . . . , no, no! It's been a long time since I had so much of the English language spoke at me. I ain't used to it."[2]

If theater is to be effective, it has to mimic real-life situations, ones that audiences can relate to their contemporary lives. This scene does exactly that! Jeremiah's hesitant response portrays a parallel issue in twenty-first-century American culture. Today's issue is found in parents who cannot understand the language of their children's teachers, their educational jargon! It all sounds like indiscernible babble, sometimes near to bringing forth Johnson's response . . . laughter!

Parents of school-age children have become accustomed to the public school establishment's story line. For years, beginning with their children's time in early elementary school, they have been unable to understand the *ed speak* (those words and acronyms teachers and administrators routinely babble) at back-to-school nights: "Values clarification, self-esteem enhancement, gender equity, word-attack skills, phonemic awareness, common core, modern this or that." It's all mumbo jumbo! Jeremiah Johnson might say of parents: "They ain't used to it!"

A common outcome of this circumstance is that parents end up feeling incompetent and unqualified to play a role in their children's schooling. They can't see if or where they could possibly fit into such a confusing system, one they can't understand. But the truth is that parents *are* competent, and eminently so. This is a statement many parents might find difficult to believe, as no one, particularly their children's teachers, tells them this. "They ain't used to it!"

Athletics and Education . . . Related?

As the experiences of those who work with university athletes have shown, many of these young people enter their universities absent an understanding of how to be university *students*. Many also are absent the confidence necessary to effectively attend to their studies. They've learned how to *do* sports, but not how to *do* academics.

NCAA Division I and II universities are required to provide educational support services for their interscholastic athletes. Student Athlete Support Services staffs are charged with the task of helping young student-athletes be successful in the second part, becoming good *students*. As was described in chapter 8, some begin by showing these young athletes that the sports psychology principles they use on the field can also be applied to their academics. As athletes are among the most skilled at applying their physical, visual, and emotional natures (to their sports), they grasp quickly how these can be applied to their studies through Making Up Crap strategies and others that make use of their unique skill sets.

The MUC strategies show them the power their unique life-related experiences have for learning. They come to understand that the *unknown* can be learned rather easily by attaching it to something that is *known*, and particularly something that is known uniquely by them. Once they *see* this relationship clearly and understand how it can empower their academic abilities, the *lights go on* and they gain a confidence that can change their perspective on their personal power to learn. They super-charge their own learning!

The Answer to the Snail's Question

What was that about anyway?! The goal of this book has been twofold: First, it is to show how everyone has uniquely God-given emotional, physical, and visual powers, and that these are the very assets that are the *most* important in learning. The language skills that you possess might be less than you'd like them to be. And you can work on that. But you have three powerful abilities that you are probably not using, or maybe even don't know how to use. You are a physical, visual, and emotional being! If you apply these three human skill sets to your learning experiences, you will enhance your learning by a multiple far exceeding three!

Additionally, the principles for achieving an excellent *athletic* performance apply to helping you to achieve an excellent *academic* performance. An Ideal Performance State is achievable in both, through the same principles! And here's the best part: you already have everything you need to begin super-charging your learning. Whether a workout junkie or a couch potato, this works for you!

A second goal of this book is to show you, if you are a parent, that you have a tangible and dynamic role to play in helping to bring about these same outcomes for your children. You no longer have to accept the paradigm that your children's education has to be taken over, in its entirety, by any outside agency. There *is* a place for you, and it is critically important that you seize it. Complaining about the educational circumstances in the schools may be a good form of catharsis, but that is all it is. If you desire to make an impact and effect a positive change for your child's education, now and in the future, YOU must act!

Parents, Time to Take *Your* Place!

Begin using the learning/remembering strategies discussed in these pages with your children, on a *regular* basis. Additionally, begin using the strategies that all good coaches use with their players. A good coach both *tells* and *shows* players how they can *become* great, and then coaches the skill sets for the player to achieve their greatness—a little of both Uncle Costanzo and Dr. Phil. For parents, encouraging academic growth and success in their children is no different.

As has been mentioned, there is a benefit for parents who help their children learn via a Making Up Crap approach . . . they learn new things also! And age is no barrier to this parental takeaway. A brain-research scientist explains the phenomenon:

> At any age the brain is subject to improvement, Dr. Michael Merzenich, professor emeritus from the University of California, San Francisco, and a longtime researcher of brain plasticity, tells Newsmax Health: It's plastic and you can improve your faculties at any age. But it's more and more important that you do that to maintain yourself in the middle and toward the end of life.[3]

So here's an additional inducement for parents who help their children with their schoolwork via MUC. It helps you too! Studies have shown that the "use it or lose it" maxim is correct regarding declining mental abilities being associated with aging. If you do not use (exercise) your brain as you get older, brain functioning declines more rapidly than if you do. So parents, by exercising *your* brains while helping your children exercise theirs, you come out a winner too!

A Word about Words

Throughout each of the preceding chapters, the intent has been to portray the uniquely God-given genomic powers that each of you possesses: to *visualize, physically express,* and *feel.* Within this context, words have been characterized as holding a somewhat secondary status, in contrast to what they can generate in us. However, it is a fine line. In relation to MUC, words are *critically* important for anyone who considers applying the strategies described herein. Words define, are the bedrock, and are the critical initial step in this process.

In her inspiring book, *Reading God's Mind: His Thoughts for Every Life Situation,* Dottie Eichhorn nicely captures the essence of the centrality of words: "Our words reveal our hearts—what we think and feel within. Before we speak, we need to think about what we are going to say. Once the words leave our mouths, we can't take them back. They are out there. Words are powerful. They can have a positive or negative impact upon a person."[4]

In Making Up Crap, the strategy is to tie your powerful emotional, physical, and visual reactions to words. In many cases, the *words* are what you are trying to learn/remember, so they are central in the process. Words will always play a large part in learning because they are the symbols for everything that is learned. The emphasis given to emotional, physical, and visual skills is meant to show that these three give the power to animate words, so that they may be learned and remembered more efficiently and strongly.

Just as Ms. Eichhorn entreats us "to think about what we are going to say" in our everyday lives, the selection of specific words that one chooses to use in the Making Up Crap process is also an important task. The words that work best, as you know by now, are those that have the greatest *visual, emotional,* and *physical* power for *your* remembering dynamic. As in life, choose carefully for best results!

Payton's Insight: *The* Critical Additive

Walter Payton played running back for the Chicago Bears from the late 1970s through the mid-1980s. Back then, Coach Mike Ditka described Walter as not only the best player he'd ever coached but also the best person. In summing up the source of his greatness, Ditka said, "Well, you didn't have to coach Walter. I mean, what you had to do for Walter is provide enough opportunities. You had to give him enough touches. You had to get the ball in his hands as a receiver or a runner, and then he would make the other stuff happen. You know, I would be the greatest fool in the world to say, 'Oh, I had anything to do with his . . . No!' *Walter's greatness came from Walter*"[5] (emphasis added).

When a Chicago reporter asked Payton what the *one* ingredient was that accounted for his success as an NFL running back, the response he offered befitted what one saw in his on-field play. Payton told the reporter that virtually all of the players come to the NFL with fairly equivalent physical size and playing skills. The difference that made some great and others average was mental attitude, the mind-set that they *chose* when they played the game.

In chapter 2, the human genome was given a good deal of attention, that unique package of traits providing human beings their ability of *controlled* thought. As mentioned, super-charged learning is really *genomic* learning . . . the result of how humans are put together. As a consequence of a uniquely Creator-constructed genome, human beings are able to learn through means within their own control, through making choices. No other animal on earth has the ability to learn by making choices, to the extent that other animals have the capacity for choice and learning at all.

Being physically bigger-faster-stronger is not really what makes one football player better than another. Certainly physical size, strength, and speed are necessary ingredients for athletic success, but they are not the most important ingredients. Attitude is the *critical additive*! And if mental attitude is of such great importance to athletic success, it is just as important in other human endeavors, not the least of which is learning. Parents need to teach their children that, right up there with content-material learning, learning to gain and keep a strong mental attitude is of equal importance.

The MUC strategies presented herein are a powerful additive for student learning, and parents can and should play a role in helping their children understand and use them in their schooling. In addition, the psychology-for-success strategies discussed in chapter 8 are of equivalent value for *all* learners. Parents who would help their children to become the best that they can be as students would do well to help them adopt and apply these to other aspects of their lives.

This is the answer to the snail's question: "So what was that all about?" It has been about parents helping their children achieve a new success in their formal schooling, about becoming super-charged learners. *This* is what that was all about.

Notes

1. "Kingston Trio's Very Last Performance Together," https://www.youtube.com/watch?v=8c3Tjk4Ck0c.
2. *Jeremiah Johnson*, Warner Bros., 1972.
3. NewsmaxHealth.net, "Fight Brain Decline Every Day," February 13, 2012, http://www.newsmax-health.net/headline_health/Fight_Brain_Decline/2012/02/13/433481.html.
4. Dottie Eichhorn, *Reading God's Mind: His Thoughts for Every Life Situation* (Enumclaw, WA: WinePress Publishing, 2011), 223.
5. "Mike Ditka on Walter Payton," https://www.youtube.com/watch?v=SV0elYiLgXc.

About the Author

Dr. Richard J. Giordano worked for over twenty-five years in public education as a teacher and secondary school principal. He currently works with elite university student-athletes in helping them make progress toward graduation while maintaining their athletic eligibility. Through his book, *Super-Charged Learning*, he now makes the strategies he teaches to athletes available to people of all ages, and parents of K–12 and college-age students in particular.

DATE DUE			

Bib#560440